A YEAR OFF...
A YEAR ON?

Acknowledgments

The publisher acknowledges permission to quote from the alternative prospectuses of several universities and is particularly grateful to the students' unions of Durham University, the University of Exeter, Cambridge University and the University of Manchester Institute of Science and Technology.

Whilst every effort has been made to accurately update the text with the help of most of the organisations mentioned, we are keen to know of any errors that should be amended in the next edition.

Enquiries

When writing to organisations listed in this book, you are advised to enclose a stamped addressed envelope with any enquiry or application. When writing to organisations abroad, you should send an international reply coupon (obtainable from any post office).

A YEAR OFF...
A YEAR ON?

A guide to jobs, voluntary service,
conservation projects and working
holidays in the UK and overseas during
your education

Student Helpbook Series

CRAC

© Hobsons Publishing PLC, 1987, 1989, 1992, 1993

First edition published as *While You Wait*, 1969
New edition published as *Time Between*, 1977
New edition 1980
Completely revised as *A Year Off*, 1983
New edition published as *A Year Off . . . A Year On?*, 1985
New edition 1987
Completely revised 1989
New edition 1992
New edition 1993

ISBN 1 85324 781 2

CRAC

The Careers Research and Advisory Centre (CRAC) is a registered educational charity. Hobsons Publishing PLC produces CRAC publications under exclusive licence and royalty agreements.

Printed in England by Clays Ltd, St Ives plc

Ref 0126/v10qq/E/JC

CONTENTS

1 • TAKING OFF

Using time out as preparation for a job . . .

'A year off', 'a year out' and 'time out' are phrases which most students or students-to-be understand. They mean a break from studying of up to 12 months, a year's relief from the grind of academic work before going up to college or university, or a year (or less) between graduating and taking up a permanent job.

When the first edition of this book was published it was fashionable to take a break from study, to go off to Europe or the United States on an extended holiday, back-packing, taking an occasional job when the money ran out, working on a farm or factory to get work experience. The next edition, called *Time Between*, carried the idea further with ideas for working on a kibbutz, in social work, going on adventure holidays.

When undergraduates, sixth-formers or graduates present themselves for interview, it can still be a great advantage, a real asset, to say 'Oh yes, I had a year off and . . .'.

Employers considering graduate applications look for something different, something extra in a candidate. Similarly, admissions tutors in universities are impressed by people who have had the courage, the independence, the foresight, the initiative to take a year off and do something else. The extra experience and the maturity which a job, or travel, or a period of voluntary service can bring, impresses tutors as it does employers.

It can't be too highly emphasised, therefore, that a 'year

off', or a 'year out', linked to work experience and vocational preparation, is seen by employers as being a very important qualification for a job.

For these – and other – reasons, Hobsons' guide to opportunities for work, for travel and for voluntary service is now published in a new revised and enlarged edition, suitable, we hope, for the needs of young people in the 1990s who are looking for useful ways to spend their 'year off'.

The book provides information on the many opportunities for work and service available to people at different stages in their education. Some will be 16–18 year-olds still at school: for them, experience of the working world or holiday opportunities for taking part in a voluntary project with other young people of different nationalities can develop the self-confidence and sense of purpose which are so important for their personal development. Others will be school-leavers with time to spare before beginning a course of higher education or starting a career. Others will be students who want to vary their academic study with a period of involvement in the community, either immediately after graduating or in some cases in the middle of their academic course. At whatever stage it is undertaken, this period is not just a way of passing the time while waiting for something more important to happen: it is an integral part of each individual's development and education in the widest sense.

'A year off' should not be thought of as a student option – something to be tried and left behind when real work begins. Community service, which is a part of many student year-off experiences, continues throughout one's life. In this sense, therefore, people of all ages and at all stages of their education will find information and a contact which they can use to volunteer themselves for voluntary service, a part-time job, a leisure activity, a holiday experience.

In this new edition of *A Year Off... A Year On?*, new material, contacts and ideas have been added on vacation jobs – throughout the year – as these can be as fruitful for career, income and personal development as any other aspect of taking time away from study.

In the book, three terms are used to describe voluntary work. The phrase *short-term* is used for periods up to three months; *medium-term* for up to 12 months, and *long-term* for periods of 12 months and over.

It should not be thought that there is any real distinction between 'work' and 'service', or between 'paid' and 'voluntary' work. Financially, some 'voluntary' workers receive more than 'paid' workers. In any case, every job involves 'working', whether it is paid or voluntary.

2 • BRIDGING THE GAP

Janet Bond looks at the advantages of taking 'time out' and some of the possibilities

When interviewing a group of recent graduates, I was struck by the fact that half of them had not followed the traditional career path through school, college, job – without a break. Half the people I talked to had found a gap in the fence. They'd taken 'time out' – a month, six months, a year, and in a tremendous variety of part-time, full-time and vacation jobs.

None seemed to have been any worse off for the break. In fact, the opposite. In terms of self-confidence and maturity they had gained a lot.

Is it a 'good' thing to take time out?

The first of these had travelled to the USA, entering a career in finance when she returned. The second had worked in a variety of temporary jobs and as a voluntary counsellor for divided families, before going into a local authority social services department. Another had a short, unsuccessful spell of postgraduate work, gave it up, hitchhiked round Europe and then managed to get into marketing via a spell as a sales representative. Others in the group had worked on a kibbutz, on a Marks & Spencer counter, visited Australia (with farm jobs to pay their way), and so on.

Their experiences raise the question of whether it can be beneficial, in terms of personal development, to have a gap between graduation and starting a career. The benefits of a year's break between school and university are now fairly widely accepted, but is there a case for taking time during a degree course – to travel, to try out different types of work, or to follow up an interest or hobby? Is there the risk of being labelled a 'dropout'?

'A year out enables you to get off the escalator of study', according to a senior recruitment manager. 'It can be very important for a young person's emotional and personal development and maturity. It's best if they do something unusual – hitchhiking round the world, for example – and if they earn enough money to pay their own way.'

Terry Wilson, a university industrial placement tutor, said much the same thing. 'If students know that their degrees are leading to a career, and they have made all the necessary arrangements before taking a year off – well and good. It may be their last chance to do so for many, many years. But a gap can also be totally unplanned. Graduates don't know how to use their degrees, and think that if they just go off for a while, everything will fall into place when they come back.'

Problems The trouble with taking time off, or getting a vacation job that extends into a year off, without any clear ideas for the future, is that when a decision is made, it may be the wrong time of year to apply for the next stage of education or training. If you are planning further study you should try to make the necessary arrangements well in advance. Students who wish to go into permanent employment, rather than further training after their break, will find it more difficult to plan ahead, but it is still worth trying to get as much information as possible in advance, and to keep in touch with the university careers service.

Attitudes of employers towards graduates who have taken a break vary a lot. However, the candidate's degree discipline is likely to be less important than overall personal qualities, so a period of time which has been used to broaden the individual's experience can be of great use.

What do employers think?

A lot depends on the career you intend to pursue. Attitudes are changing, even in accountancy. Counsellors at the Institute of Chartered Accountants say that 'a break of a year wouldn't be a disadvantage at all'. However, the Institute says that 'it's very much a personal thing – depending on the individual firm'.

From the point of view of an employer, it is worth considering whether we sometimes put young people into positions of responsibility before they are quite ready for them in this country. In the United States, it is common for graduates not to begin work until their mid-twenties after a prolonged period of training and education. Perhaps in Britain we should follow this pattern, with a year off being seen as an important part of an individual's personal development.

The transition from full-time education to employment – at whatever age it happens – can be difficult. Some people need time to adjust, and a period of travel, or of temporary work, may give them the necessary breathing space.

Despite the horror stories about youth unemployment, the job market is varied and plentiful – if you don't mind doing dirty, boring and short-term jobs. Many students find jobs in pubs, hotels or shops, covering for staff absences and holidays, and these can turn into permanent jobs. Others apply to local councils for jobs in parks, recreation centres and on children's play schemes. There's

What are the possibilities?

a host of jobs with local cleaning companies and secretarial agencies.

How do they do it? Most students approach the landlord, the council or the shop manager direct – by calling on the phone or, better still, by calling in person. Here are some real possibilities.

Try the business world

Being a 'temp' is one of the most readily available jobs, especially in the summer season. This means you should take an intensive typing course to fit yourself for the job. Better still, see if you can get on a word-processing course at a local FE college in the evenings – this gives you more than typing skills. All major towns and cities have 'temp agencies', or use the *Yellow Pages*, or go to the local employment office.

Tough jobs are on building sites as labourers, or in warehouses as humpers and carriers. The work is hard and you should be fit. Most of these jobs are filled by a personal call to the site or warehouse.

Another area is industrial cleaning. This means joining a cleaning agency which cleans offices, factories, workshops, colleges, schools, etc. Most agencies employ part-time staff and there always seem to be vacancies.

Seasonal jobs come before the Christmas shopping spree with the big – and small – stores looking for extra hands. Every shop from Harrods to Charlie's Cornerstore is on the lookout for people who can count, be polite under pressure and are prepared to work long hours. Some people do this full-time! As well as Marks & Spencer and the rest, there are other companies with warehouse staff, drivers, carriers, shelf-fillers, packers and other tasks – all needing new hands.

If you have a polite manner, clerical experience and some skill with a foreign language, try travel agencies. They have 'rush' periods too, but with staff holidays they are often on the lookout for replacement staff.

If you can stand children for long periods – not the same as taking Aunty Alice's baby in a pram for a walk around the park – there are agencies in London and other cities which look for young assistants. Mothers' helps, nannies, skivvies – the names vary but the jobs can be interesting although tough for a different reason: the pressure of coping with the demands of children over a longish period. Mothers know what I mean.

Working with children

Many British graduates – especially those with sporting inclinations – have been recruited for Camp America or Involvement Volunteers in Australia. The 'summer camp' idea is catching on in Britain too, and there are possibilities as general assistants, kitchen-hands, dogsbodies, cleaners – and, of course, wardens and activity instructors. This is where the PE knowledge comes in handy. The work isn't highly paid but it can be great fun, although seasonal, unless you can get a job at a ski centre in Europe.

Part-time jobs are also available at Butlins and other summer camps. The season can last from May to September, so that much of your year off could be spent at one of the rivals to 'Hi De Hi'. Other possibilities are sports and activity centres: again, if you have knowledge and skill in canoeing, climbing, fell-walking, camping, archery, caving, swimming, athletics or team games, your chances of pulling an instructor's job, or an assistant to one, are immensely improved.

Holiday jobs

Students who are taking courses relating to hotels and catering have little difficulty in getting a job, full-time or part-time, permanent or temporary. The demand

Hotels, catering, meals

increases as the British tourist trade improves. However, for students the hours tend to be long and the pay unappealing. If you take a job in a hotel, make sure that it observes the rules and regulations (or recommendations) of the Wages Council for the catering industry.

Farming

There is some summer farm work, but mechanisation has led to the loss of jobs. It's not as easy as it was in Hardy's Wessex days. Fruit-picking is seasonal but the opportunities are better. Again, earnings are low and it can be backbreaking.

Try employment agencies

Public and private employment agencies in all major towns and cities have details of temporary jobs which don't always tempt the unemployed. They may be suitable for you. Otherwise call in at your local council offices where there may be temporary jobs covering for staff absences. Social services centres often have openings for adventure-playground leaders and staff, and for assistants in residential homes for the elderly or handicapped.

Au pairs

Working as an au pair is a cost-effective way of spending some time getting to know a country, its language and customs. In Canada and the United States au pair programmes, with their emphasis as much on community involvement as on childcare, offer opportunities to both sexes. Au pair stays in a variety of European countries are usually for a minimum of six months; stays in the USA generally last 12 months. Families look for students in the age range of 18 to 30.

Community

In recent years voluntary work in the community has become more and more important. Voluntary work can be of great value, personally as well as to the people you help. Projects can last from three months to a year; the work generally involves working with people in need, such as the disabled, poor, handicapped, disadvantaged, sick and the young. Volunteers generally pay their own fares. Ages 18 to 30 + are looked for.

On the kibbutz

Israel offers opportunities to students who wish to spend time on a variety of work, from six weeks to a year. Volunteers, who pay their own travel costs, should be between 18 and 32.

Teaching

There are opportunities in EFL (English as a foreign language) teaching in the UK and overseas, particularly in Spain, France and Italy. Preference is given to students with an A-level or degree in a foreign language who show the qualities that make a teacher.

Voluntary work

There are many voluntary organisations that offer a very wide range of projects. These can run from three to 12 months, and are based in Europe, Asia, Africa and the Americas. The best guidebook is *Working Holidays*, published by the Central Bureau for Educational Visits and Exchanges.

Whatever attracts you, it is absolutely essential to think hard about why you want a year off, because it is an important decision. If you do intend to seize the opportunity to enjoy the freedom of no ties for a year, it is vital to plan ahead for the years after a year off, and thus prepare for entry to a higher education course or a job. But, whatever happens, it is unlikely that you will regret taking time off to escape – for a time – the shackles of full-time education or a full-time job.

3 • MY WAY

Personal stories of students who took a 'year off' to do something different

Camping in America

On the last day of my degree course, I flew to the state of Maine in the USA. I had decided earlier that there was one thing I must do when I finished college: visit the USA. I used the Camp America organisation and eventually ended up teaching ceramics, to children of all ages, in a summer camp in New England.

by Samantha Jayaram

One great advantage was the fact that my flight was paid as part of my wages. On top of that, I was fed, housed and paid pocket money. From my 'year off', I gained first-hand experience of the American people, their culture, and their way of life.

Some of my experiences were not particularly welcome, such as a minor car accident when, half-way through an eight-week stint on camp, I broke my collarbone. However, this meant I experienced the American health system at first hand too.

Luckily, my broken collarbone healed fairly quickly and I was able to travel around America with a pair of British camp counsellors who I'd met on camp. On our journey through the USA we stopped to stay at the homes of American counsellors who I'd met on camp. Their welcome was always hospitable and we enjoyed experiencing the American family way of life.

Air-boat rafting on a Florida swamp; a hurricane in New Orleans; a visit to Disneyworld – these were some of my experiences of travelling around America. Altogether I spent three months in the country; the camp work was often difficult and tiring, but the experiences I enjoyed, the American sights and scenery, and the people I met all made it worthwhile.

When I returned from America, I still didn't have a really clear idea of what I wanted to do. I took a temporary job in the local authority as a Liaison Officer in the Treasury department. 'Liaison Officer' is a title given to people behind glass-fronted inquiry desks in local authorities. I dealt with the public and their hundreds of inquiries and thousands of complaints. The job was at times tedious and repetitive, but it was also beneficial because I had to co-operate and work in an office environment with people of all ages.

Another important aspect of doing a job that you may not particularly feel is your ideal vocation, is that it clarifies and concentrates your mind into defining your aims in life and doing something about it. More importantly, it helps you to appreciate the elusive first 'proper' job that you finally manage to obtain.

This isn't the end of the story of a 'year off'. I'd decided on a postgraduate course but had to wait another year to start it. So one year became two, and I spent this time living and working in Paris as an au pair, but that's another story...

For information about Camp America, contact the organisers: Camp America, 37a Queen's Gate, London SW7 5HR (telephone: 071 589 3223).

Au pair

by Alysoun
Owen

Being a firm believer that the best way to see a country is not to Inter-rail through it with a pack on your back, but to be a resident for a few months, I decided to make good use of 'time off'. I was lucky to have both a gap year between school and further study, and a year off after taking my degree. In addition, I enjoyed visits abroad during the long vacations. These were all paid for by temporary work in the UK; the fact that one's travel is self-financed also adds to the feeling of independence.

After A-levels, I spent six months as an au pair with a family that lived in the French Alps. My main objective was to bring my spoken French up to my written standard. Living with a family in a foreign country can be difficult, but if you are prepared to be flexible, being an au pair is probably the best way of experiencing foreign kitchen-sink drama at close quarters. I found my family through personal contacts and I think this, rather than agency placings, is the preferable and safer way of finding suitable work. Stories of au pair slave labour are not totally unfounded. An au pair is not a glorified house-keeper and any contract should stipulate exactly what is required. Au pairs earn only between £30 and £40 a week, but there are usually opportunities to teach English to locals, and this supplements your income.

I was very fortunate in my situation. I had to look after two young boys when their parents were away. I was asked to speak English to them. I had plenty of free time and the family arranged for me to have French literature and tourism lessons at the local lycée which brought me into contact with other young people; there is a danger that au pairing can be a lonely occupation. France has an excellent network of correspondence courses similar to those of the Open University, and so I enrolled on a linguistics course with Dijon University.

Au pairing is fun, but it can be tiring and tiresome. However, if you are young and not too averse to children, it's a valuable way to spend time. Many of the old clichés about au pair-seducing employers and girls running off into the night in despair can be true; furthermore, there can be traumatic consequences if your employer fails to declare your residency.

Having a year off meant that once at university I had no problems of homesickness and was fairly independent, and dare I say it, more mature than most of those coming straight from school, who were only just realising the delights of being sick over the college gardens after an over-indulgent drinking bout.

Italian bliss and French rail

I spent a year out of education after finishing my degree in Latin at London University. I had decided that I needed some time off after the strain of finals and before deciding on any academic course or full-time employment. I spent the summer working for a large department store in London in their hosiery department. This was hard work, especially during the sales when shop hours were long. Two months of selling 'nylons with lycra' finished me off completely, so I left for Italy.

The idea of spending some time abroad really appealed to me. Out of sheer luck, and with no practical experience, I acquired a job teaching English in an institute in Milan. This was a most enjoyable time. I taught spoken English to adults of varying abilities and ages. There is always plenty of demand for teachers whose native language is English, and private lessons are an excellent way of providing extra finances. I managed to learn some Italian as well as making some good friends.

Then came my second job. I left Italy for France, where I became employed by SNCF on the French railways. I was based in Biarritz, the surfing capital of the south west. My main job there was as a telephonist giving information on fares, timetables, recent applications and reservations. This was a hectic time and in complete contrast to the previous months of Italian bliss.

I then spent one month travelling by train around Europe on an Inter-Rail. This is an excellent way to see Europe. I decided to make the most of the opportunity for unlimited travel and I visited places as diverse as Norway and Gibraltar, Liechtenstein and the Greek islands. However, trains in southern Europe are often heavily delayed, crowded and a general health hazard, especially during the summer months.

by Sheila Harrington

The time I spent abroad made me all the keener to put off any ideas of a 'proper' job and to return to full-time education.

Parisian experience

My year out was spent in Paris as an English assistant, a compulsory part of my French and English degree. Initially I found myself homeless for two weeks, lugging round huge suitcases bearing my few essentials. Along with another assistant I bought the early morning papers each day and searched for an apartment. We were lucky and were able to move into a two-room furnished apartment on the outskirts of the city; we were unlucky in that we had to share a lumpy double brass bed for the whole of our stay. Negotiating and signing the contract was quite interesting with our shaky French.

by Inga Brooks

Because we had debts, we lived frugally for months, filling our time visiting free exhibitions, museums and going to matinees at the pictures at reduced prices. We got to know the cheapest Chinese restaurants in town and met lots of au pairs, who all had horror stories about some of the families they had worked for. Two of them had gone to France directly after their A-levels, not knowing a word of French. These courageous women lasted the year too. We all frequented a groovy jazz club, Le Caveau de la Huchette, cheap on weekdays, and Le Saint, a disco free to women, both situated on the Left Bank. Otherwise we whiled away our time wandering the streets.

I worked a meagre 12 hours a week in a secondary school where half the lesson was spent getting the kids to get rid of their gum or put away their Walkmans, or even sit still for ten minutes. Most of the kids at the school were from immigrant worker families, so I was teaching Vietnamese, Italians, Turks and Germans, which helped show me the other side of Paris to the chic Champs-Elysées. Teaching improved my French, as I was obliged to speak it in the staffroom, canteen and, of course, the classroom.

One of the highspots of my time was taking part in an education demonstration. Students and lecturers took to the streets, halting traffic in central Paris for most of the day. Another was speeding around the Périphérique at 140 km an hour on the back of a teacher's 1,000 cc Kawasaki, which was a good way to wake up in the morning!

I look back on my year with nostalgia and feel that I could survive in any big foreign city having done it successfully in Paris.

Communal living in a kibbutz

One of the most popular student tactics of 'getting away from it all' is to turn one's back on Europe and to head for commune life. A kibbutz (Hebrew meaning 'group') is a society in which everything (apart from personal possessions) is held in common. The guiding principles of a kibbutz are the desire to establish an egalitarian society and to undertake tasks important to Israel's development. Set up by the pioneering Jews who escaped from Europe in the 1930s and 1940s, the kibbutzim were originally self-sufficient agricultural communities, social rather than religious. Today, when the founding ideals are less relevant, many young kibbutzim retain their farming traditions but supplement this with money-making commercial businesses and hotels which serve a wider community.

by Alysoun Owen

Although not quite the ideal egalitarian community, kibbutzim are a way of experiencing communal and family togetherness, something which many Western societies have allowed to become diluted. Some kibbutzim still have children's houses, but it is now more common for children to sleep at home with their parents. All cars are held in common and meals are taken together in the dining hall. Kibbutzim vary and some are very prosperous, but the ideals remain the same. In theory, all members (a committee vets those asking to join or marry-in) are equal, receive equal pay and take part in all general chores (cooking, cleaning, farming).

Kibbutz volunteers work alongside the kibbutzniks. They receive board and lodging, free cigarettes and a small allowance to spend in the kibbutz shop in exchange for their labour and the opportunity to take part in this unique cultural experience.

I stayed for six weeks (usually the minimum period) in

the upper Galilee close to Nazareth. Work was in the kitchen from six in the morning until two, and sometimes in the evening, but afternoons were free. The kibbutz had a library, small zoo, swimming pool and floodlit tennis courts as well as a volunteer bar and club. The enjoyment gained from one's time on a kibbutz is due in great part to what you make of it. Overtures towards friendships with the kibbutzniks must come from volunteers; they are wary of visitors passing through, and British volunteers have a heavily sullied reputation for being idle and unruly.

If you want to explore a different way of living, to experience months of sun and learn more about Israel, then a kibbutz is an ideal starting base. Be prepared for spartan living conditions; you also have to earn respect through hard work.

The kibbutzim welcome volunteers from all over the globe. The majority seem to be British, South African and Dutch. Living in the midst of the Galilee, in a predominantly Arab area of the country, I was ideally placed to travel out on day trips to Nazareth, Tiberius and Haifa and to witness life in different parts of the community. The kibbutz arranged visits and if you stay long enough, these can be overnight stays. I arranged to leave my belongings on the kibbutz and to travel to Jerusalem for two weeks. The kibbutzniks look favourably on people wishing to undertake personal travel while in Israel.

Kibbutzim are fascinating places to stay; they are a unique way of experiencing a life which has specific aims and routines, where work but also play – both individual and group – is very important. A student experience of this kind is not expensive; no money is needed whilst on the kibbutz. Your main expenditure is the return air fare to Israel.

Off to the USA

by Gill Higgins

The greatest attraction of a year out for me was the challenge that it posed. I had no concrete plans but still went ahead with deferring my entry to university in the hope that something would turn up.

The first summer was spent earning money and writing letters. The jobs I had were not exactly glamorous: a car park attendant at a flower show, a sales assistant behind the sausage counter at Littlewoods and an apple-picker in Kent, but they did keep the money coming in. Unfortunately I was not getting much of a response to the letters I'd sent, and so as a consolation I blew most of my earnings on a holiday in Cyprus.

However, when I arrived back there was a reply from some family friends who lived in America, offering me a job in Los Angeles. They wanted me to fly out within two weeks and take up residence with them for five months. This meant that, although I was working for them, I could go there without having to get a work permit. I understand now, though, that it is all far stricter, and I was lucky enough to get away with just a probing interview at the airport.

The job I had was a mixture of duties. I looked after their eight year-old daughter, accompanied Mrs Oakland on speaking engagements and was an assistant to Mr Oakland who owned his own construction corporation. This involved driving around to various banks and offices, composing letters and making excuses on the telephone. None of the work was particularly demanding, but the day was always full and there were always new things to be learnt with regard to the different way the Americans run their businesses and homes.

I was given a Lotus Esprit to run around in, which was great fun but not without its mishaps, such as running out of gasoline in the fast lane of the freeway the first week I was there, having a tyre blowout, locking myself out of the car one cold dark night in Westwood, and being stopped by the police, sent to court and fined for having my headlamps on full beam.

It was definitely invaluable to experience the American way of life, which I was fully able to do by living with a family. Occasions such as Thanksgiving, Hallowe'en and the Presidential elections were particularly memorable, as were the dozen or so games of baseball I played for the local women's team – all of which we lost.

I returned to England in March and decided it was about time I applied for a job that would prove useful to the degree I was about to take, which was in the human sciences. I therefore enquired about working in hospitals and research centres in London, and in the meantime worked in the Argos store in my home town, Shrewsbury.

Eventually I was offered a job at the National Heart Hospital in central London, working in the Medical Records Department. Although the work itself was not terribly exciting, it was an interesting environment to be in and I was able to see two open-heart operations carried out. I'd probably faint if I saw them now, but at the time it obviously appealed.

That job finished in September, which gave me a few weeks before starting my degree. I definitely think that the year was time well spent, giving me greater confidence and independence, and an insatiable urge to travel and try out new things. It was also worthwhile in the sense that it opened my eyes to the opportunities in life, and their accompanying difficulties but ample rewards.

The American alternative

If the prospect of visiting the States has ever appealed to you, then why not use BUNAC's Work America scheme to get a job out there as a starting point for your year out? My job, which I was fortunate to get whilst still on English soil by using the Work America job directory and was much coveted because it had accommodation 'thrown in', was as a front desk receptionist in a lodge belonging to a company which ran raft trips down several rivers in Maine.

by Rosalind Camp

Wealthy Bostonians and New Yorkers take a couple of days out to experience the challenge of class IV and V river rapids (for the uninitiated this means ten-foot waves, steep falls and turbulent water). Of course it's not all hard work. There is a guide in each raft, chosen for their ability to entertain as much as their survival skills, whilst the steak cookout, three-bean salads and coffee are served at lunchtime with the professional expertise of Americans running a lucrative business, rather than with the rough, wilderness manner one would expect.

Unlike previous summer jobs I'd had, I found that I was charged with far more responsibility. As there were few employees actually working in the office, I was soon punching reservations into the computer, ordering new supplies of T-shirts or photographic equipment, and selling the river trips over the phone with a much admired English accent. Being English proved to be advantageous time and time again, both to me and my employer, who sent me under the guise of a dumb tourist to quiz other rafting companies about their operations.

Working arrangements were also far more flexible than I had anticipated. Towards the end of the summer, when trips were smaller and the phones less busy, one of the raft guides would leap into the office and suggest water-skiing, whereupon some of us would leave work for a few hours and 'party' in style, in a speedboat on the lake.

Being near Canada provided several opportunities to travel over the border to Quebec, a beautiful European-style city with French cafés and cobbled streets, and then when I finished my job I was able to stay with American students in Boston; a fascinating compact seaport, combining historic architecture and museums with a modern, growing culture.

Finally, after visiting friends in Cape Cod, I flew to California for three weeks. It was possible to travel the 3,000 miles across country in a Greyhound coach for a paltry $59.00 or, better still, to acquire a 'drive-away' car, placed by an American who is moving house or going on holiday, in the hands of a transporting company who will find them someone to drive it from A to B. A deposit and proof of being 21 are required, but you are allowed quite a generous time limit to enable sightseeing. Time was a major factor determining my mode of travel, however, as I wanted to visit Mexico, San Diego and LA. My last weekend in the States was spent in Hollywood, where banks served their customers with coffee and cookies, restaurants were frequently ex-directory and where I found a shop which sold water; no alcohol or coffee, just 147 different types of water at $2.00 a glass.

To be eligible for the Work America programme, you need to prove that you will be spending, or have just spent, a year in further education, but apply to the scheme quickly, either by finding a friend over there who will 'sponsor' you or by finding a job, since the 3,000 places were filled by April last year.

For details on Work America, or for information on working in American summer camps, write to BUNAC, 16 Bowling Green Lane, London EC1R 0BD.

Switzerland and Germany

Take one year off and double it up. The result is two years off. I have been one of the fortunate ones to have profited from this double opportunity. My first year out was taken straight from school. Since my birthday is late in the academic year I have always felt younger than my year group at school, and hence this year off gave me the chance to 'catch up' with my equals. Instead of considering these 12 months as a perennial holiday I was determined to use this free time to my advantage. I was intent on studying languages, so it was an automatic decision to go to Europe and polish up my spoken languages.

by Sonya
MacMahon

Whilst still in England I fixed myself up with a job in Switzerland, working as a chambermaid. This I found with the help of the Jobs in the Alps agency, which seeks employment for students, primarily in the hotel/catering fields. Working in a hotel is quite a good idea, since they usually provide accommodation (though grotty) and the money is good (especially with generous tips). This was the first time I had travelled to a foreign place by myself and naturally I felt frightened (my main worry was actually finding the town and arriving safely), but at the same time I felt independent. From now on I alone was responsible for my welfare.

In all, I spent four months in Switzerland before coming back to the security of friends and relatives. These four months were a sometimes painful period of self-examination and self-awareness. My experiences, however, made me revise my rather preconditioned attitudes from home and led me on to self-improvement. Above all I came back home having more respect for foreigners, instead of being prejudiced towards them. Having to work with Yugoslavs, Portuguese and Italians taught me to be more flexible in my outlook. Whether I actually learnt a lot of French is a different matter!

After a brief time at home I went to Germany and stayed with friends. Since I had permanent contact with Germans my language certainly improved. Although I did not look for a job at this time, I did spend my time positively. My major achievement was learning to type, which has been a real bonus to me ever since. I would recommend this to everyone.

My second year out was in fact a compulsory part of my degree course (German BA), which I spent in Hamburg. Although more mature, I did find this year very tough at times. Instead of being an English language assistant, which most tended to do, I found myself work experience within a German company. I sent off about 50 letters, finding the addresses in the German equivalent of the *Yellow Pages*, and my efforts bore me one hopeful reply. But that was enough, and it has in retrospect provided a springboard for my intended career.

When I set out for Hamburg I was in a totally different situation from when I set out for Switzerland. I had a job fixed up, but no accommodation. So my first few nights were spent in bed and breakfast, until I found a furnished room. A good tip for room-hunting is to go to the local university, where there will be a student accommodation bureau. The next thing I did was to get myself a bike so that I was mobile. For lengthier journeys it was worth my getting a young person's railcard, and I spent weekends travelling all round Germany, visiting towns and cities of interest. This was good fun; work on the other hand was not so easy. The most difficult part was making friends with colleagues, and trying to arrange to go out in the evenings for a drink or something. You could be chummy with them at work, but out of work they had their families or own circle of friends and were hardly interested in getting to know a newcomer. Hence the only way to make friends was to join a club of some sort and thereby mix with people who had the same interest or hobby as myself. And, to be honest, it was only after several months that I established firm contacts.

It was an upward struggle right up to the point when my year off was drawing to a close, and the irony of the whole thing is that I was only beginning to feel at home in the country when it was time to leave. Perhaps the best thing about my year in Germany was that I experienced the country and its people at first hand and began to understand its customs. Previously, I had visited the country merely during the summer/winter holidays and the vacation spirit had always tinted my attitude. My year out shattered many of my beliefs. I now realise the true nature of things, rather than viewing them through rose-coloured spectacles.

Tulips and bulbs in Amsterdam and other European jaunts

by Mark Jensen

When I graduated, I had no idea about the kind of work I wanted to go into. The prospect of settling into a career seemed daunting. Having gone straight from school into higher education, I was reluctant to make another long-term commitment. So I decided to spend a year working and travelling abroad before doing anything else.

Along with some friends, I took a seasonal job in a packing factory in Holland. The work involved putting flower bulbs into cardboard boxes ready for export. The workforce was made up of about 200 young Irish, Scottish and English people, who all lived in company-owned accommodation next to the factory.

The hours were long and the work was monotonous. But the evenings and weekends made it worthwhile. Exploring Amsterdam and other towns made a welcome break from the production line. I spent two months at the factory before going on to France.

I had managed to arrange a job picking grapes in the Beaujolais region. Grape-picking was hard work. We began each day at seven and worked through until six, with a two-hour break for lunch. Picking went on seven days a week until the harvest was completed. The weather was excellent; very hot almost every day. Because the pay was low, the farmers compensated by providing masses of French cuisine and plenty of wine. After three weeks and a short stay in Lyons, I returned to England.

In order to earn some money for the next trip, I spent two months working for a temporary employment agency. Having no skills to offer, I did the lowest-paid jobs. Typical of these was a stint of nightshifts spent loading lorries at a Securicor parcel depot. Other assign-

ments included filling in the potholes left by horses'
hooves on Chepstow Racecourse.

Just after Christmas, along with another graduate who
had been in Holland, I went to Spain. We had no plans
to find work, just to travel around. By staying in hostels,
using the buses and eating in local bars, we managed
to visit and explore six different towns and cities in southern Spain. After a hectic but hugely enjoyable three
weeks I went back to England and the employment
agency.

After more lorry-loading and pothole-filling, I boarded
a coach for Greece. From Athens I took a ferry to Crete.
I hoped to find work on the island and stay for some
months. I tried speculative visits to orange, olive and
tomato growers, various hotels, a sawmill and a cement
factory. However, in each case the fruit harvest was over,
or they were fully staffed, or work would be available if
I came back in a month or two. Although other people
do find work in Crete, I never did get a job there. Even
so, by living very cheaply, such as sleeping on beaches
and living on eggs, I managed to stay six weeks before
getting the bus back home.

My year off was now almost up. I began looking for a
permanent job in England, where I could actively use
my academic qualifications. But selling the benefits of
my year off to a potential employer was more difficult
than I expected. I felt that I had learned a good deal of
self-reliance and taken the opportunity to do something different. I eventually went into the commercial
world and took a worthwhile and interesting job in
London. Not all employers are likely to be impressed
by a job applicant who has 'a year spent travelling
and working abroad' on their CV; but it did me no harm
at all.

From a personal point of view, had I gone straight into a permanent job on leaving higher education I may well have regretted it in years to come. My year out gave me a complete break from everything I'd done before. Another opportunity may not be so easy to come by.

Improving your skills

When faced with an unscheduled and unwelcome year **by Karen** off between A-levels and university I opted to do an **Whitlock** intensive one-year secretarial course at my local college of further education. Not the most exciting choice I suppose, but I thoroughly enjoyed it and in retrospect it was a very sensible decision.

The course I chose was the LCC Private Secretary's Certificate. In theory two A-levels were the minimum entrance requirements, but quite a few of my fellow secretaries had failed their 'A's and none the less been accepted. Those that wished could devote three hours a week to studying for an extra A-level.

Although shorthand and typing (up to RSA III) were a large part of the course, we also had time for some academic studies. 'Communications' taught us the importance of clear, concise language in everyday business situations, including letters, reports, staff announcements and presentations. 'Background to business' provided a foundation in economics, most useful for those like me who had never studied it at school. Finally, 'Office practice' taught us everything from streamlining a filing system to conducting committee meetings.

If I had planned to have a year off I suppose I might have done something a little more adventurous – sold ice-creams in Monte Carlo or cycled across the Andes. As it was, I broadened my horizons across a typewriter keyboard and do not regret it in the least. Office skills are something that will serve you well, whatever career you eventually end up in, and they always look good on a CV. Also, of course, they provide a useful source of income over those long university vacations.

If you are looking for something to do in your year out, you could sign up for a secretarial course.

A shadow university student

by Darren Bugg

My year off was unusual in that it was also a year on. By this I mean that I decided to spend a year in a university environment, although not studying for a degree.

I took my A-levels at 19 and left school with a vague idea of wanting to work in the media, although with no definite plans. I already had experience of working voluntarily for a radio station and I'd written articles for local newspapers. I therefore applied to do a university course in human studies, which included options in communication studies.

My A-level results were much better than I'd hoped and I made a total rethink of my plans. I decided to take a year off and begin a law degree course the following year, which I thought would be a good general degree for a career in the media.

The first thing I did was to contact my local education authority to make sure that I would still be entitled to a grant for my law course. Then I contacted the university department to find out if they would allow me to remain a notional student on their course, despite the fact that I intended to leave after one year. Both my local education authority and my department were in agreement, so I was in the lucky position of being technically a student, although with no exams to take and plenty of time to pursue other things.

Added to this, my course was very flexible and I was able to organise my own syllabus to a large extent. I must stress at this stage that anyone thinking of spending their year off in the same way as I did must first ensure that their education authority agrees. I was lucky to have a very generous authority, but many would refuse to pay three years' grant to anyone who knowingly intended to change universities after a year. Another point to stress is that many college departments would not agree to this plan. A school friend of mine tried to do the same thing and was politely requested to leave his course. The essential thing to do is get permission in writing from your college and your local education authority.

My year off was spent mainly learning to be a student. This is not as silly as it might sound. I decided to acquire all the skills I would need for my law degree course. I learned how to type. How to cook. How to use the library (this really is a skill as any law student will tell you).

I learned how to take good lecture notes. How to prepare for a tutorial. How to get the most out of lectures. How to survive on a student grant. How to handle difficult landlords. How to stay awake during philosophy lectures! Most importantly, I made frequent visits to my future Alma Mater, so that when I began my degree the following year I was already well acquainted with the university and the city. For anyone who intends to take a year off I would strongly recommend that they make at least four or five visits to their future college to get to know the place. This is invaluable during the first few months when trying to search out the cheapest shops, best pubs, sleaziest clubs, or the only place in town to sell beer at four in the morning (usually curry houses).

The rest of my time was spent working for the university magazine and doing various voluntary work. I worked for a hospital radio station as a presenter and as a football commentator. I worked for the local animal welfare group, helping with publicity and organising campaigns. I became involved with a local football team as their supporters' club press and publicity officer. I decided to buy a camera and learn about photography. After much studying of techniques, I embarked on a mission exploring Britain's northern cities in an attempt to capture on film the atmosphere of these towns. I even managed to sell one of my photographs to a national newspaper for the princely sum of £250, although I risked my life in a riot to get the picture.

By the time I began my degree, I already felt like a student and I had a lot more confidence than others on the course who were living away from home for the first time. I was also two years older than most of my contemporaries and this gave me added confidence and experience of life. Most importantly, I was ready to study from day one. While my fellow students were wasting their first few months either feeling homesick or in the traditional freshers' drunken stupor, I was keen and ready to learn.

Archaeology and travel

Only after I knew my A-level results did I decide to make a fresh university application and have a year off. This was the first of many junctures at which I realised I really did have a choice. I decided to stay at home at least until Christmas to accommodate the round of university interviews. This provided the first block of my year, a period in which to try and get something done, as well as to plan and prepare what I might do with the rest of the year. Initially I sent off for endless year-off schemes: teaching English in Eastern Europe; summer camps in the States; voluntary work in Africa ... However, I ended up doing my own thing.

by Adrian Green

In August I went on a Mesolithic (10,000 years BC) excavation in Yorkshire for the month. We found flint, bone, worked wood, and investigated settlement theories and landscape archaeology. We determined the shoreline of a Mesolithic lake in a present-day peat bog. I also met amazing people who would regale me with their exotic life stories in the pit or down the pub.

During the autumn I undertook voluntary work at Leicester Jewry Wall Museum, doing part-time work and odd jobs for the rest of the week. Throughout the year I was able to earn cash from gardening, painting, decorating, laying lawns, pruning apple trees ... all of which were conducive to thought, if nothing else. Before that year I had never done any archaeology, but by Christmas I had been fieldwalking, picking up pottery shards, artefacts and glass, done some processing work and produced diagrams for a publication.

I undertook other voluntary work with the small town museum at Market Harborough. The museum has a collection of over 800 Leicestershire slate headstone rubbings, from the sixteenth through to the nineteenth century. Fascinating for their typography, symbolism and stylised detail, particularly for the earlier localised 'folk art' designs, these rubbings had been produced by the remarkable 90 year-old Harold Jones, one of the many remarkable people I met through the museums. The museum wanted a catalogue produced of these rubbings, a project that escalated into a publication and earned me a contract as Assistant Curator. The curatorial work involved mounting exhibitions, working with school groups, special needs students and senior citizens. In my first university vacation I was back working at the museum, editing the reminiscences of a local farmer for publication. The year out continues to haunt me! The museum work allowed me to earn some money, which financed a month in Russia in March/April, and a month in the deep south of the States in July. More importantly, I met interesting people, contacts and friends who have outlasted the year.

The Russian trip was the exotic element of my year. My visa and my stay with people in St Petersburg and Moscow were arranged through a family friend. I travelled alone by train from Leicester to St Petersburg. The train journey through Holland, Germany, Poland, White Russia and the Baltic States was fabulous. Travelling alone makes it easier to start talking to people, and I had a brilliant journey to Warsaw with two Dutch professors going on a dirty weekend, and a drunk Polish sea-captain who was returning from the Rio de Janeiro carnival. From Warsaw to St Petersburg I shared a couchette with a rather large Russian lady named Poleena. When we arrived in St Petersburg the train was 12 hours late and the student I was staying with was not at the station. Poleena invited me to her flat for breakfast. I think she wanted me to carry her bags of western electrical goods purchased in Poland.

The Russian trip was full of remarkable people and memories. The Russian public transport, shopping – or the lack of it, an Armenian meal, Moscow restaurants, opera, ballet, student parties, vodka bouts... I had a 'wonderful' – one of the two words a Ukranian student who showed me round Moscow spoke – time, and plan to return this summer, travelling with my new friend in St Petersburg to his relations at Lake Baikal on the Mongolian border.

The year put a useful distance between the sixth form and university, enabling me to return to education with a fresh approach and enthusiasm for study. I realised that I had choices and learned how to get things done, though not without problems. Perhaps overcoming these is part of the experience. Personally, I found it productive to break the year into chunks, to focus on what I was doing and arrange what I might be doing next. The result was rewarding museum work, an introduction to archae-ology, and travel in France, Russia and the States. The first evening at university I was with people who had spent gap years in Japan, teaching in Barcelona and having art exhibitions in New York and I was amazed to find they were equally impressed with my tales of Russia, gravestones and gardening.

Au pairing in Europe

by Rowan
Unsworth

Deciding to take a year off before plunging into the heady world of higher education was not a difficult decision to make at the time. In fact, the promise of a year away from exams, textbooks and broken deadlines had kept me going through sixth-form college. It was reassuring to know that the next year would provide the chance to do what I wanted to do, an academic breathing space if you like. Lots of people, I later found, do lots of very different things with this gift year, and the sky is certainly the limit, but from the first I knew that I wanted to work abroad, and, if I could, earn myself some money for the long slog ahead. Europe seemed to be the ideal location: foreign, but not too far from home if disaster struck – and I certainly wanted to improve my French. So I decided to look for a position as an au pair with a French family.

The search began about six months before I wanted to leave, in order to have lots of time to change my mind and not to let the juiciest jobs slip through my fingers. Copies of *The Lady* magazine began to pile high on my desk. Scanning the local papers became a highly refined skill, and before long my stack of neatly photocopied CVs had all but vanished. I had a fairly strong idea of the sort of job that I was looking for. I knew, for example, that I wouldn't be able to cope with more than a couple of children. So after a while I put my name down with an employment agency that specialised in placing personnel abroad, in case any jobs that matched my specifications were to pass their way. In the end this proved to be a wise move, as they found me what seemed to be the ideal placement almost straight away, leaving me free to plan revision schedules and worry over past papers instead. Fine.

With exams over, my year off had finally arrived. By the end of June I had contacted the family in question, written polite rejection letters to all the others and paid the agency. By the end of July I was dragging my suitcase off the train at St Lazare, Paris, desperate to find a phone as I had missed my connection. Not an auspicious start. I arrived at midnight, very apologetically, to greet the family who intended to employ me for the next 12 months.

The trial fortnight passed smoothly; the family were charming, and I was willing to do anything to make their lives easier. In retrospect, this was where things started to go wrong. Nothing nightmarish, but a series of 'amendments' to our initial agreement (a revised wage, increased responsibilities, etc) that started off as favours to the family but ended up as fairly blatant exploitation. At which point, of course, I should have got in touch with someone from the agency to reinforce my position, but, unfortunately, the company involved had forgotten to include the relevant sheet of contacts in the paperwork they had sent to me. So, basically, I had to cope with the changes myself, and I had a pretty bad time. On the brighter side, living with a new family was a great experience. My French improved and I was learning a lot about how to cope with people. But whereas my relationship with the children gradually got better, my view of their parents worsened. By Christmas I'd had enough. I left awfully messily, and put the whole episode down as experience.

Luckily, I fell on my feet. A friend of the family recommended me to a colleague who needed someone to fill in while their usual au pair took time off. As my journey back home took me through Belgium, I was invited to meet them and decide whether or not to take up their offer. I met the child I would be looking after, the people I would have to live with, even the dog. They spelt out what they would want me to do and what they would give me in return. It was all written down on paper for me to refer back to whenever I wanted. This was the right way to do it. If the previous family had known to express their expectations of me earlier, and if I had insisted on some form of written contract, then perhaps I wouldn't have been so easy to exploit and it might have worked out better than it did. This time we all knew what we were doing, the family were friendly and were used to having help around the home, and the three months that I spent in Brussels turned into the high point of my year off.

Living in a capital city was wonderful. I was near enough to a metro station to get around and had an understanding family to explain the ins and outs of city life and to introduce me to people and to places worth visiting. As my previous job had been in an isolated village without public transport, I had been left without any people of my own age to meet, which became unbearably lonely. I was concerned that this was not to happen again. However, the Belgian family had already considered this, and insisted that they pay for language classes for me. This provided a good excuse to explore a different part of the city as well as an unlimited source of interesting people. As a class we would go out for meals, to the cinema, and on day trips to other parts of Belgium. As we got to know one another better, firmer friendships developed, and a group of us would meet up in our free time to explore Brussels, and to find out more about the people who live there. An added bonus was that the family I worked for were heavily involved with the European Parliament, and could introduce me to the countless students who work there as assistants, which meant that I could meet people who spoke the same language as myself. What a relief! The three months sped by far too quickly and, before I knew where I was, the original au pair was due to return and I was saying good-bye.

There you are – two ways of spending a year as an au pair in Europe. Basically, the good way and the not-so-good way. The importance of meeting the people for whom you are going to work seems to spell itself out, but apart from that clear objectives are useful, along with a sense of fun. Although I chose to work with children to earn some money, you don't have to restrict yourself to domestic work to get along... your year off is really what you choose to make it.

Open ticket to Australia

by Geraldine Ismail

Well, I had arrived. After nine months' hard labour and six months' intensive applying – not to mention the work entailed in comforting my distraught parents – I had an apartment on Bondi Beach, Sydney and a 12-month work visa all of my own. What more could a girl want? A job maybe! The air fare plus the bond on accommodation and forward rent had taken almost every penny of my precisely calculated finances (meant to furnish my year out) and I had arrived only eight days ago. In addition, I could not shake the worst summer cold in history; the result of a short stay in Bali that had left me sunburnt and disillusioned. Yes, there were paradise beaches, but I had needed a peg on my nose.

Sydney in winter is cold, wet and very windy but I was determined not to be dragged down. With a will of iron and nerves of steel I landed the perfect job by walking into a hotel and asking for work. After a week as a chambermaid I was promoted to head receptionist and became the manager's general assistant. I met innumerable people, including pop stars, the weather was picking up and, to top it all, I was earning three times as much as I could in England.

By Christmas the heat was intense and I had visited every New South Wales landmark. I had been mesmerised by the wonders of the Sydney Opera House, spent a weekend at the Guinness and Oysters festival with more Irish people than I knew existed and probably knew Sydney better than your average 'ocker' (genuine Australian). I was restless and it was time to move onwards and, after South Australia, upwards.

The Bus Australia open ticket gave me 12 months' unlimited travel around Australia. I probably spent more time on coaches than I did doing any other single thing. Melbourne was hot, sunny, rainy and dismal all in the same day. Bustling, yet lacking the obvious friendliness of Sydney. Adelaide was very green and the inhabitants truly knew how to appreciate good food and music, open-air festivals and Bring Your Own picnics.

I travelled on to Coober Pedy, where I was bowled over by the way of life of the inhabitants. Translated from the aboriginal the name means 'white fellows' hole in the ground', and describes how the inhabitants live in underground dugouts to shelter from the uncomfortable, constant 50° heat. You can well imagine the surrounding outback if you recall the movie *Mad Max III*, the majority of which was filmed there. Why on earth would anybody choose to live in such an unattractive, dry, barren place where even the water has to be brought into the town? The answer is that Coober Pedy is the opal mining centre of the world and you can earn a small fortune if you set up in an area most wouldn't live in for all the Castlemaine XXXX in Oz. I think it was probably the rats in the underground mine fronting as a hostel and the fact that you could not go above ground at all between 11 am and 5 pm, unless you wanted to get sunstroke, that forced my hasty retreat and yet another interminably long bus journey.

Next stop Uluru. The national park encompassing the world's largest and most extraordinary formation: Ayers Rock. Truly magnificent. At sunrise, from the site at Yulara, I watched it stretch and yawn as it changed from dull grey to the most vibrant red. The view from the top is equally impressive but the descent is not one to be favoured. The towering height, howling wind and blazing sun make it dangerous for any but the most cautious of climbers. As mysterious and interesting as the rock itself is the aboriginal mythology that surrounds the site. The aborigines now officially own the park and it has been their decision which areas of the base, paintings, carvings and water holes are accessible to the public.

After the beauty and magnificence of Ayers Rock, I believed nothing would quite match up. How wrong I was proved to be by a week spent on the Great Barrier Reef scuba-diving, snorkelling and floating around on a catamaran just off Cairns. It is difficult to describe how it felt to be swimming some hundreds of feet below the surface alongside innumerable types of anonymous sea-life. So close to nature and yet never once did it enter my mind that the water might be inhabited by deadly sharks and was most definitely home to venomous scorpion fish and deadly box jellyfish. Perhaps most memorable is the astonishingly multicoloured coral that makes up the mass of the reef. And, of course, I will never forget how my diving instructor was continually pulling me down to prevent me rising uncontrollably to the surface because the weight of my belt was insufficient in comparison to my body weight. What a compliment!

Well, after more of the same: islands, sun, reefs and fish on the northern tip of Queensland, a relaxing time was needed, so off I trundled to Kuranda. With a population of only 500, peace and quiet was assured. The trip from Cairns to Kuranda entails a 30 km train journey on the historic 1888 line through the most spectacular scenery. My most poignant memory is of the guitarist Mark, who played every evening to a crowd of howling travellers in the central social point between our log cabins in the midst of the rainforest. Dire Straits' 'Romeo and Juliet' has ever since held fond memories for me. The days were spent mooching around the craft market and shops and taking short, organised jungle walks.

Five months and 8,000 km after leaving Sydney, more

than 12 months and heaven knows how many kilometres since leaving England, it was time to decide whether to return. For me the decision was all too easy. I had seen what I could while in Australia, but now I had to look ahead and finish my education.

This short account illustrates only parts of my year off. It was far from plain sailing. At the time it was true that if you were willing to do anything you could generally get work and earn amounts far in excess of those available in England, but the down side is that you are far from home and those you love. Living from a rucksack, sleeping where you drop or find a cheap bed – whichever comes first – and wearing the same six or seven items of clothing for the duration of your journey can really make you appreciate the home comforts you've left behind.

Camp life in the USA

by Jo Selby

You've decided to take a year off. The only problem is what are you going to do. How do you arrange it? Can you afford it? These were just some of the questions going through my head when I decided to take a year off in 1990. After numerous trips to the careers library, I finally stumbled on a brochure for GAP Activities Ltd who offer a number of placements all over the world. I filled in an application form stating the placements of my choice and waited nervously for an interview. It came and went and after being asked how I would solve world poverty and homelessness, I began to lose hope. But another application form arrived, this time for a place called Sargent Camp in New Hampshire. I was told I had to be hyper-fit, love children and like the general outdoors life. So for about four months I tried getting fit amidst sorting out visas, travellers cheques and flights. I was given the names and addresses of two other Gappers and plucked up the courage to phone them; probably one of the best moves I made. They too had no idea what to expect. We presumed we would be helping out behind the scenes at a camp that taught children and old age pensioners outward bound! How wrong we were proved to be.

The big day finally came when we were to travel to the States. Luckily I was travelling out with Tom, another Gapper. (I'd recommend finding a travelling companion if you can.) We went through periods of quiet and nervous hysterics and just hoped that there would be someone to meet us at Boston airport. There was and we found ourselves at Sargent Camp in the middle of New Hampshire on a site of about 120 square kms. Piers, the other English boy, arrived soon after and there we were with 13 American staff with whom we were to be living for three months. We were told our accommodation would be dormitories with bunk-beds, but it turned out to be a seventeenth-century farmhouse that was spacious and comfortable.

First of all we had two weeks' intensive training and discovered that we would actually be teaching, not just helping around the camp. Each week around 40 to 120 children, usually aged between 10 and 14, would visit the camp from school. Rather than being purely for outward bound, the children's visit was broadly educational. They learned how to work as a group; to solve problems; and were taught about the natural world around them. We taught activities such as ecology, orienteering, astronomy, canoeing, group-building activities and hiking. Also included were presentations, night hikes and a ropes course that was 30 feet high.

Every week we were each put in charge of a group of 10 to 12 children and we had charge of them all day and evening, including meal-times. If you had a tough group this was both mentally and physically tiring, but was amazingly rewarding as well. To see a group arguing and fighting on the first day, and on the last day having a group hug and working together, made even the worst week worthwhile.

A typical day began at 8 am with breakfast, when we were introduced to the word of the day for which we had a special chant that built up over the week. We went on to the activities, which varied daily: crossing rivers on cable bridges, building campfires or finding our way back to the camp after being dropped off by minibus with all the kids blindfolded. After returning for lunch we would again set off for activities, which could involve trying to get the whole group across quicksand or a treasure hunt in the forest. Supper followed and then evening activities such as astronomy or searching for other groups in pitch blackness, fondly named 'Predator Prey'. At 9 pm the children went to their cabins and we had finished for the day. Once or twice a week duties also included overnight supervision, which meant sleeping in the cabins with often up to 40 children.

Even the staff had to learn to work as a group; I can see myself that first week sitting back and letting others take charge, something that at the end I would never have let happen. I became very close to the other Gappers, that special bond between us always clear and I still keep in contact with them. All the Americans offered to have us to stay whenever we wanted during our travelling. I learned to live and work with the same people, to be with them 24 hours a day knowing that at times I just needed to be by myself. If you needed a break from the children, there were jobs to be done around the camp, such as nightwatch and resource. Resource included jobs like tidying and ropes course maintenance. We all got a chance to be camp nightwatch person.

Our staff-training days usually involved doing something really mad, such as going off a death slide from a bridge into a river 40 feet below! My first time on the ropes course I couldn't make it to the top death slide. I felt an amazing exhilaration being cheered all the way down from the platform by a group of children. To me it seemed like conquering Everest! My greatest memory is of the change in me over the three months. I went unsure of myself, straight from school. I learnt a great deal from my workmates and left that much more confident of my own abilities. I was learning new things every day, either from the children, their teachers, who had practical criticism and praise to offer, or my fellow interns (as we were known). As well as teaching, we had a chance to travel at the weekends. I went to Maine, Boston, Connecticut and Vermont.

While I was there I was introduced to many different aspects of American culture: their food; their customs, such as Thanksgiving, which I experienced when we were kindly invited into a family; and their massive consumption of Ben and Jerry's ice-cream, which I still crave. It was a sad occasion when we finished and all of us went our separate ways. I was due to go travelling for a month or so after staying in Boston. I took a Greyhound bus into the centre of New York; something I probably wouldn't have done when I first arrived in the US three months earlier.

Unfortunately I had all my luggage stolen from a friend's car, so I had to return home early. A sad end to what has been one of the best times of my life for experience, fun and personal growth. I'm now at Newcastle University but Sargent Camp, far away in New Hampshire, still holds a certain part of my heart. I still feel that bond with the people I met there, as we were the 'Interns of Fall 1991'.

Working round Australia

by Sarah Bartle

In June 1989, with my A-levels and school-life at last behind me, I could finally concentrate on what I had been daydreaming about for so long. I had been promising myself that I would go travelling before I started the next stretch of hard study, namely my law degree.

I cannot claim to be the first in my family to carry out such an expedition as I was, in fact, following the example of my older sister Jules, as I have in many things in life.

When she was 18 my pioneering sister travelled to Australia and New Zealand and on her return she convinced me that to travel before your degree is the only way to go. In fact, there are pros and cons to both options. When you travel before your degree it can be your first real departure from home, your parents and pets, etc. If you travel alone, it can be lonely and at times a bit daunting and your naïvety can sometimes be a problem. But it is a new and eye-opening experience and once you find that you are quite capable of steering yourself relatively trouble-free round a foreign country, starting your life at university seems a doddle.

Be warned: one real danger is that you will like travelling so much that you will be tempted to go after your degree as well!

Warning number two: you will be tempted with notions of remaining in paradise and abandoning England for ever, but the sobering thought of a degree normally brings you back to Earth and England.

How do you go about it? Well, making a deferred entry to university is a good idea: it gives you the security of knowing that you actually have a place to come back to, without having to frantically negotiate UCCA and PCAS clearing procedures.

Finance is the major headache. Take any job going as soon as possible. I started working in Waitrose stacking shelves, but soon moved on to a less strenuous and better paid office job. However, believe it or not, saving money is not as simple as it should be ... The date I was due to set off was forever being postponed. Finally, in January 1990 I had enough saved for a ticket and the compulsory funds required by Australia for a visitor's visa – about £1,000 (to show that I wouldn't starve while I was in their country).

I bought a 'round the world' ticket from Trailfinders in Earls Court, London, for just under £1,000. Armed with this I had a choice of travelling to various specified cities worldwide by going one way round the world or the other. I opted for America first, New Zealand and then Australia. The best thing about these tickets is that you can stay in each country as long as you like, all that is required is that you fly with the airline(s) specified on your ticket. Although you have to book your flights in advance to give a rough framework, you can change the flight dates at any time and as often as you like.

I was fortunate in that I could claim some kind of contact in nearly all the places I visited, whether a relative or a vague acquaintance my sister had made while on her travels and with whom she had happily exchanged addresses in the certain knowledge that their paths would never cross again, ever. Well, not until little sister came onto the scene. At first I was extremely embarrassed to call up these people and make contact with them, but I soon became quite blasé when I realised that as travellers themselves they were only too happy to help and offer support. If you can't use a similar network, don't despair. Youth hostels are great meeting places and you soon make enough contacts to see you round the world twice over and in places not even on your route.

I took some sterling travellers cheques with me, but I mainly survived on plastic; Visa really is worldwide. Although wandering around a city late at night in search of a Visa cashpoint can be an enlightening experience and, of course, once you have gleefully located the only Visa cashpoint in the whole of Cairns, the computer system is down. So take a little cash, but not so much that you are haunted by fears of letting your bag out of your sight for a second.

Probably my biggest mistake was to go equipped with a suitcase. If, like me, you have serious problems lifting your case onto the weighing machine at Gatwick, reconsider before it is too late. You will buy so much stuff on your way that you don't want to be setting off with a full load. And face the fact, you are not going to wear your bargain English T-shirt in Sydney, where you do not want to be identified as British and where the T-shirts are infinitely more gaudy. My suitcase became the bane of my life. It restricted my freedom and I was embarrassed to be seen with such an enormous specimen, but at least it was a good opening line for conversations. 'I can't lift my suitcase, can you help me?' The saga reached its climax when I was told by a bus driver in New Zealand to send the whole thing back to England by sea mail and start again. But by this time my suitcase and I were inseparable. I was going to get around the world with that suitcase, if it was the last thing I did.

Getting work on the way round was much simpler than I had anticipated. Although I had a visitor's visa and was therefore working illegally, no one ever asked me to produce a working visa. I aimed low. Washing-up seemed a viable option, so I spent four agonising days in Perth loitering in various cafés that I thought looked like they might be traveller-friendly and in need of a washer-upper.

Finally, I plucked up courage and asked. It was easy: the first café I asked offered me a job for two weeks. I was paid the minimum wage, which was then $5 an hour. This unexpected coup paid for a trip to Monkey Mia to swim with wild dolphins (the best thing I did).

I then managed to get a job on a sheep farm some five-and-a-half-hours' drive south-east of Perth. I talked my way into this job with the help of a friend, but there are agencies (in the Australian equivalent of the *Yellow Pages*) that offer vacancies for farm work to travellers. The job stirred up all my romantic notions of bringing in the sheep on horseback and camping in the bush – real 'flying doctors' stuff (if you ever saw it on TV). In reality I was to cook and clean for the farmer and his son and help with the sheep when needed. Incidentally, the sheep were rounded up by motorbike and jeep, which proved to be just as much fun as with horses. It was a well-paid job; I ended up with approximately $500 for 3–4 weeks' work, but it was hard work. While I was there it was 'tailing' time for the lambs and de-maggoting for the ewes. It was my first time on a 'real' farm and I found the new-born lambs irresistible. I wanted to take them all home with me. But the farmhouse already had its own half-grown lambo, which was convinced it was half-dog, half-human but didn't conform to any notion of toilet-training and one was more than enough.

One phenomenon I encountered was that Australians and New Zealanders don't believe they have a winter. I was told it would be only a few weeks of rain: in fact it's two months of rain and even snow. Unfortunately, because Australians don't believe in winter, they don't believe in central heating or heating of any kind, so my thick jumper was well used. There I was believing that I was leaving behind a typically bad summer in England for constant sunshine, when I actually found myself hearing in disbelief that my parents were enjoying better weather in England than I was in Australia...Oh well, one consolation was that I managed a skiing trip in the Blue Mountains south of Sydney.

PS If you don't want a round the world ticket, a single ticket to Sydney, for example, can be just as good. There is an excellent bus system in Australia that offers special travel tickets with unlimited stop-offs for each region. The youth hostels are great places for catching lifts and sharing cars but be careful if you are travelling on your own.

PPS If you think you are escaping everybody by going away, don't believe it. I came out of a café in Sydney and walked straight into a friend I hadn't seen for two years and who I didn't even know was in Australia.

My Gap placement in India

by Sarah Selby

Although I wanted to travel in my year off, I knew that I would feel guilty simply backpacking around the world or bumming on a beach somewhere without doing something constructive. GAP Activities Ltd provide placements worldwide for a duration of 4–6 months teaching or doing social work and this seemed to be the obvious answer. Developing countries had far more appeal for me and I finally decided upon India.

After a fairly lighthearted interview there was an anxious wait until I heard that I had a placement starting in August to teach music at a boarding school in Himachal Pradesh – in the Himalayan foothills. The short time after A-levels was made frantic by packing rehearsals, injections and fond farewells. I boarded the plane feeling both excitement and trepidation. The organisation had paired me off with another girl, whom I had met only once before arriving at the airport. This was part of the challenge: being thrown in the deep end for six months with someone I might not have got on with. Luckily I got on extremely well with Georgie and know that we will always be friends, having been through a lot together.

Arriving in Delhi at 1 am was an eye-opener. Lengthy delays at the airport soon initiated us into the Indian pace of life. Even at that time the heat and smell on walking outside were oppressive, but were quickly forgotten as we were surrounded by numerous shouting rickshaw drivers – something we were soon to become accustomed to.

The drive to the station was very interesting, as we swerved constantly to avoid dogs and cows lying oblivious in the road and were deafened by the noise from the horns on every vehicle. To drive in India you need three things: good brakes, a good horn and a strong heart, as the traffic rules are obviously there to be broken.

After a wait at the station we finally caught the 4 am train to Kalka. This was followed by a bus trip up a road with terrifying Himalayan hairpin bends, during which people were frequently sick. The Himachal scenery made a pleasant change from the hustle and bustle of Delhi, and eventually we made it to the Lawrence School, Sanawar.

Our first day at the school was spent becoming familiar with the campus, which at 6,702 square metres was huge, and had spectacular views. We were continually inundated by keen pupils with very confusing names eager to arrange piano lessons.

Our task was to teach piano and some singing to 8–18 year-olds, and I also taught some recorder and flute. The main requirement was for patience, as few pupils had a great aptitude for music. It took us a while to get used to being called 'Ma'am'.

Our greatest challenge was to take the entire school (800 pupils in all) for singing rehearsals of their school song and 'Abide With Me', as only a very small minority had any concept of pitch, and the aim of many of the pupils was to see how long we could keep our tempers! The school celebrated its Founder's Day mid-term and my partner and I were asked to produce some songs for a concert with the 'preppers'. About 70 children wanted to join in and, not having the heart to turn any away, we allowed them all to sing. It was a great thrill to see them on the day, all crammed on stage in their best clothes and stage make-up doing the actions to 'Consider Yourself' from *Oliver*!

As the school was in such a remote area, I met only one other Westerner in four months. This gave me a great opportunity to integrate with the local people and to get to know their customs. I even attempted to learn Hindi and weaving from the local village girls at the school's rural centre.

Divali, the Festival of Lights, took place in October and we were lucky enough to be invited to the celebrations, where I was brave enough to don a sari. All day we were slightly on edge due to the continuous snap of firecrackers designed to make a tremendous noise rather than be spectacular to look at.

Invitations to three weddings came our way. These were very colourful affairs, where we had great fun eating Indian style with our right hands from disposable leaf plates, not forgetting to belch loudly at the end to show our appreciation of the meal!

Some weekends we were able to travel and we visited such places as Manali and Simla.

At the end of term we gave a concert to the school and also arranged a carol concert for the pupils. This was a great success, as we had taught carols to students of different religions: Hindus, Muslims and Sikhs. It was very sad when the time came to leave the school in December, as we had made so many friends.

As it had started to get quite cold at the school, woolly socks and log fires being a must, we decided to head south immediately. In some towns there were problems resulting from the destruction of the mosque at Ayodyha, but the headmaster had given us advice on the places to avoid. We did once make an unscheduled halt for the night because there was a curfew in one town on the journey.

We stopped off at Delhi, Khajuraho, where there were wonderful temples, the caves of Ajanta and Ellora en route to Goa, where we spent Christmas.

There we met up with about 20 other Gappers, all with very different teaching experiences. Their students included Tibetan monks, poor children in Manali and sports students in Bangalore. Some had worked with Mother Theresa in Calcutta. This was a relaxing time spent on palm strewn beaches enjoying the local drink, feni. However, it didn't seem like Christmas, eating noodles and sunbathing!

After New Year we had to drag ourselves away, as there were many places in India still to be visited. By this time I was aware of the need to keep a tight rein on spending and set myself a daily budget of 150 rupees (approximately £3!). I had bought a month's Indrail Pass in England, for which I was grateful, so the £3 was for just my living costs. I became adept at finding hotels costing 20 rupees (50p) per night, including bedbugs and communal washing facilities, and also a skilled bargainer when buying food.

Our travels included Bangalore and Kerala before heading back up north on a 40-hour train journey full of incidents. (I won't complain about BR again!) The Taj Mahal at Agra was even more spectacular in reality than I had imagined. We spent 15 days travelling on, enjoying the colourful life of Rajastan. This included camel rides in Jaisalmer. (Typically, my camel was the only female and on heat, so it had a tendency to charge off into the desert.) The other highlight was a three-hour ride on an elephant, followed by a visit to the home of the owner, where his wife and family were very hospitable. Finally we visited Calcutta and Varanasi, the most important place of pilgrimage in India, before the time came to fly home.

Even though I looked forward to home with great

anticipation – baths, western food, no hassle from Indian men and shopping without haggling – I didn't want to leave India, having loved the friendliness of the people and the variety of things we had seen. However, the person with the well-used rucksack on the return flight was completely different from the fresh sixth-former who had flown to India six months earlier.

4 • TIME OUT

Many of the alternative prospectuses written by students and published by university and polytechnic students' unions have a section or a chapter headed 'A year off', 'Taking time off', 'Time between', 'Summer jobs', or a similar title. These articles discuss the pros and cons of interrupting the long haul from A-level to a degree qualification, with a year or so doing something else. Here, for instance, is how one alternative prospectus introduces the subject:

'Once you have finished A-levels, you may find the opportunity to hitchhike to Athens, drive across the US, pick oranges in Israel, shear sheep in Australia, perform in a French circus ring, run night shelters in Plymouth, sell clothes in Carnaby Street, or find a job as a bingo caller, interior decorator, Securicor guard or sperm donor. .

'All of these occupations have been open to students taking a year out before starting at university. This year will probably be the only time in your life when you have no responsibilities to other people, and no pressure to settle down to a career, so it is worth making the most of it!'

For the purposes of this introduction – and the book – we shall call it 'a year off' – the commonest expression used to describe the 'alternative experience'.

Timing

People take time out at various times:

1 After GCSE – a year or two in a job before going to a further education college to take an A-level or BTEC course.

2 After A-levels or Scottish Highers – a year or so immediately after leaving school, and before going on to

a higher education course in a university, polytechnic or college.

3   After graduating – when you have your first qualification (a degree, a diploma, a certificate) and a break is needed before taking a permanent job.

Whatever the timing, 'a year off' can be spent in several ways. Among them are:
- voluntary service – paid or unpaid
- workcamps – in the UK or abroad
- summer (and winter) jobs – home or abroad
- adventure holidays
- conservation work
- temporary, short-term or long-term jobs in the vacations or for longer
- study courses – here or abroad
- au pair work
- travel, expeditions, adventure holidays
- working holidays.

Whatever the timing, this book tells you something about all of these possibilities.

Getting a job   With high unemployment figures, it may be difficult to see how a student-on-the-loose can get a job – whether short-, medium- or long-term. But it is possible.

As one university student puts it:

'Even in times of high unemployment, it is still possible to find work in this country. If you are prepared to roll up your sleeves and do the dirtier, more tedious jobs, you will always be able to find something, whether the employment be as a factory worker, shop assistant, or hotel waiter/ waitress. These may not seem very exotic but, particularly if you wish to travel abroad, you will need some money, and contrary to popular belief it doesn't grow on trees.

'It can also be good experience to find out how boring and mind-bending many people's jobs are.

'Work experience can also be useful to your further career: if, for example, you are going to read law at university, a period of work in a solicitor's office will give you an excellent insight into the subject.

'If you're looking for a job in Britain, go to your Careers Advisory Service and you may be lucky. But the best way of finding a temporary job is by keeping your ear to the ground, checking the 'sit-vac' columns in your local paper, the personal columns in national papers, and foot-slogging around as many employers as possible until you hear of a vacancy somewhere.'

Another kind of work experience is in voluntary service. As the students themselves say:

Voluntary service

'Many people use their "year out" to do some socially useful work, and find it satisfying to give something back to society after receiving its benefits for the previous 18 or so years. Community Service Volunteers (CSV) is one of the largest organisations, and prospective volunteers who meet the criteria are not turned away without a place. The Voluntary Service Register lists over 100 different opportunities around Britain, and your local Volunteer Bureau, Council for Voluntary Service and Social Services Department should be able to help you.

'Voluntary work abroad is harder to find, although teaching and social work in Kenya, India or Egypt, for example, has received good reports from students. Workcamps can be very good fun and are organised in a wide range of countries. They are a cheap way of seeing another country and meeting different people. Toc H also organises voluntary work abroad. Israel is a country which attracts thousands of foreign students each year, and a stay on a kibbutz, a moshave or an archaeological dig can be arranged by Project 67. A visit to Israel can be a marvellous *experience and is not as risky as many people try to make out.'*

Or travel Another way to spend part of a year off is in travelling abroad, on a course, or in a holiday job. Here's one viewpoint:

'One of the fashionable countries at the moment is the United States. US immigration officials are not always the friendliest or the most helpful of people, and you may have difficulty getting a work permit if you want to work there, especially if you haven't got a job to go to. Jobs can be found through the Summer Employment Directory of the United States *available from Vacation Work, or by arriving and putting on your best 'English accent'. Camp America can fix you up with work as a camp counsellor in a children's summer camp for nine weeks and they pay your flight across and give you pocket money.*

'Work in Europe is easier to find. In EC countries you don't need a work permit and, if you convince your employers that you are a student, most countries will allow you six months' tax-free work. Girls can find jobs as au pairs either through contacts or through the numerous agencies. Before leaving Britain it is advisable to have a written contract or letter of invitation from the host family clearly setting out the terms of employment, remuneration, accommodation and travel. During the winter in particular, hotel work can be found through advertisements in news-papers, but don't go with any ideas that you will be free to go skiing every afternoon.'

Holiday companies Another kind of job you can get is a holiday job.

'If you can speak passable French, Spanish or Italian, then one good source of employment is holiday firms. Camping firms in particular, such as Canvas Holidays and Euro-

camp, need many young couriers to run their campsites, and the people taking a year out have a great advantage in being able to work from May until July when most other students are supposedly hard at work. Jobs in France can also be found in the directory Live and Work in France, *and for jobs all over the Continent try* Summer Jobs Abroad, *both available from Vacation Work.'*

Whether or not to take a year off is a very hard decision. Here are the pros and cons.

Student opinion

Pros – You will never have three, six or nine months handed on a plate to you again. It is a unique opportunity to opt out of the academic rat race for a breather and a reappraisal of what you plan to do next.

Cons – It is easy to be sidetracked if you fall in with people whose priorities are very different from yours.

– It is possible to get out of the habit of studying, which will make settling down to university life that much harder.

'I came straight up. Personally, I regret having been immediately siphoned into the first stages of the career machine. Temporary release will never be so easy again; nine or twelve months' respite should not be passed up lightly if you think you can use it constructively.'

'I did not have a year off, mainly because I had had the chance to travel widely with my parents in my childhood, and was anticipating a varied lifestyle during and after university.'

'Unless one has definite objectives to achieve during a year off (travel, a particular job, etc) I believe that it is of no detriment to come straight to university.'

'Acquiring a "vast personal fortune" is not a necessary prerequisite to life as a university student, and, in these times of high unemployment, finding a job and saving money

to travel is obviously fairly difficult. Independence does not necessarily come with a year out, but is something that is an obvious consequence of being a student. Provided that one can cope with that, I believe that coming straight up is not a disadvantage.'

Is it worth it? In the first place, universities like to know! If you intend to defer entry for a year, you should tell the university, polytechnic or college about your intentions. Most staff in higher education welcome it – they say over and over again that it gives students extra maturity.

It should be stressed that a year off isn't good for everyone. It certainly shouldn't be rushed into without a lot of thought. But if you have the right attitude, and you are willing to 'rough it', and do occasional menial jobs, you'll find lots of opportunities for meeting people, acquiring new interests and doing things you'll never have the chance to do again.

You should be prepared to work in a job you dislike, and with people you don't particularly like. But that's a price you pay, and your job will teach you to be aware of people's problems and difficulties, something you may not have considered before.

Further reading *Directory of Summer Jobs in Britain* edited by Susan Griffith, £7.95

Directory of Summer Jobs Abroad edited by David Woodworth, £7.95

Work Your Way Around the World edited by Susan Griffith, £9.95

Kibbutz Volunteer by John Bedford, £5.95

Summer Jobs USA, £9.95

Emplois d'Eté en France, £7.95

The International Directory of Voluntary Work by David Woodworth, £8.95

The Directory of Work and Study in Developing Countries by David Leppard, £7.95

The Directory of Jobs and Careers Abroad by David Leppard, £9.95

All these books can be obtained from Vacation Work, 9 Park End Street, Oxford OX1 1HJ (telephone: 0865 241978).

Also look for *Volunteer Work* and *Working Holidays*, both published by the Central Bureau for Educational Visits and Exchanges, Seymour Mews, London W1H 9PE.

International Understanding – sources of information on organisations that help find jobs. Published by the Department for Education, it can be obtained from bookshops.

5 • ALTERNATIVE VIEWS OF A YEAR OFF

Here are some views of a year off from students. The articles are from alternative prospectuses, published by students' unions.

The publishers are most grateful to these students' unions for permission to reproduce extracts from articles in alternative prospectuses:

Cambridge University
Durham University
University of Exeter
UMIST: University of Manchester Institute of Science and Technology

First, Durham University's view . . .

Durham University

A year out I'm reading some old prospectuses and they all seem to say, 'Yes, a year out – a good idea'. At university the atmosphere is so different that you need time to get 'experience' after school.

I think that this is less true than it was five years ago, because of the conservativeness of more and more of the universities and also the smaller opportunity for occupying a year out. Not that there isn't a *massive* number of things to do and 'experiences' to be gained. But be aware of what you *can* do, and plan to do something. A number of people who had a year out found it a waste of time since all they did was to lounge about getting the occasional job, otherwise joining the dole queue every two weeks. Unless they spent the time doing research (and places are hard to come by), scientists found that a year out made the first year a bit taxing, having forgotten all their formulae during it – obviously there is no such problem with vocational courses such as law.

Many found that doing some form of community work was satisfying and rewarding. Opportunities for such work abroad do exist but are limited. Just getting away from home and institutions can be extremely valuable. But this may make you resent the paternalistic attitude of many Durham colleges.

Certainly the year may make prioritising in the first year much easier. If you have had some experience of organising your time – ie: to get things done and to enjoy yourself, you won't get into the situation of some first years who either don't work, or work too much.

Perhaps one of the most valuable things about the year out is that it makes you think about what you want to do and not what the school or the parents want you to do. It enables you to step off the conveyor belt from GCSEs to A-levels to university, and think about what you enjoy doing, and what you don't, so that you can steer your future in the right direction.

Enough of the lecturing. If some of the above comments were pessimistic, the general impression of Durham students is that the year out was *very* useful. However the year out had always been well organised, and involved planning.

Some things Durham students have done in their year out:

   'Wait for a job I didn't get'

   'Be a postman'

   'Pose around the USA'

   'Work as a general slave'

   'I killed chickens in France'

Teaching

Working on a building-site

Working in a hotel

Inter-Railing

Taught in Thailand and then travelled in SE Asia

Some comments about the year out:

   'Good for a view on life but not for a degree'

   'Yes, it was great'

   'Very useful'

   'Useful – I think it should be compulsory'

   'It gives you a different perspective on education'

   'It was vital. It gave me an idea of what sort of environment I would like to work in in future. I made some cash and managed to save some of it, and made a lot of friends outside the educational system.'

   'Very definitely worthwhile. I'm more self-reliant and more confident. I learnt about other cultures and different ways of life. I lost my awe of academia.'

Cambridge University students have a different opinion . . .

A year off? Most students coming up to Cambridge have had a year off, although as more places are given with A-level offers, fewer are taking this time out. Many who have had a break bear witness to the great advantage of increased maturity, massive personal fortunes, opportunity to get engaged, whatever. Those who have come straight from school do not seem over-despondent at all the chances of travel, adventure, excitement and experience they have missed. As a general principle it is nice if six months, a year or two years, can be spent some time between school and retirement, thinking, doing charitable work, and/or meeting different types of people from those encountered normally.

A period before university is quite well suited to such enlightened enterprises. After university, many students owe money and are under pressure to work straight away. A year off can provide an opportunity to organise intimate and financially rewarding sponsorships with companies, while on the other hand there are no doubt those who would find it hard to return to academic commitment after so long a break.

'You will never have nine months handed on a plate to you again. It is a unique opportunity to opt out of the academic rat race for a breather and a reappraisal of what you plan to do next.'

'Unless one has definite objectives to achieve during a year off (travel, a particular job, etc) I believe that it is not detrimental to come straight to university.'

These two statements encapsulate the pros and cons. For
further information contact the Careers Service, Mill
Lane, Cambridge, for their *Jobs Before Oxbridge*.

UMIST says...

Taking a year off

The idea of taking a year off is a very attractive one for students, employers and universities alike.

Employers believe that someone who took a year or two off between A-levels and university will be more mature and have a more realistic attitude to their careers as opposed to someone who has just emerged from 16 or 17 years of continuous education.

Universities take the view that if you have gained the experience, maturity and independence which a year off gives you, then you will be able to contribute a lot more to your course. After all, it should be a collective learning process shared with other students as well as teachers.

From a student's position there are several pros and cons. You may not have the opportunity to have a year out, free of ties and pressure to succeed, ever again, so this is the time to make the most of it! It is an ideal chance to escape the academic rat race and sit back to reappraise what you want to do with your life. The style of work is very different in universities as opposed to that in schools and colleges. In both of these you are continually monitored by your teachers whereas at university the onus is on you to commit yourself to adequate study to benefit more fully from a university education. Taking time out will break down the rigours of school life and prepare you for the sort of study expected of you in university. Also the drop-out rate, which at UMIST is about 10% on average, is largely due to people who did not have the time to consider what they really wanted to do. Time out will give you that time and avoid you making a mistake which could waste a year of your life.

On the other hand, it can be very easy to be side-tracked by people who have different ideas from you but you should be able to realise what is best for you. Also, some people feel that after such a break from study it will be very difficult to settle back into that habit again. People who have taken time off find that their approach to study is actually better suited to some courses than those who have just plunged straight in.

If you do decide to take a year out then tell UCCA first. They won't be very happy if you mess them about too much, so you should make your intentions clear. You can either apply from school/college and defer entry for a year or you can apply when you are ready to go into the university system, when you have spent some time off.

If you want any more information on this subject then you should contact your local Careers Advisory Service who will be able to help you.

University of Exeter Students' Union...

'A year off'

One of the many bewildering alternatives facing you as you try to make the ultimate choice about university is going to be whether or not to take a 'year off'. Teachers and careers officers often advocate a year's break and no university would penalise you for deferred entry; on the contrary, they usually welcome people who have made this decision. So, do you chance it? I hope, with the experience of a year's break behind me, I can make the choice clearer for you by outlining the benefits and drawbacks of choosing to take a 'year off'.

The big crunch, of course, during that in-between period, is likely to be money. Primarily you will want to be self-supporting, enough at least to give you a degree of personal freedom, although you will probably continue to live at home. Money (unless your parents are generous and wealthy) means finding a job and getting a job today is often like finding a dinosaur's footprint in your back garden. Employers are unlikely to take you on for a year or less in any job that demands training, so your job range is likely to be somewhat restricted. It all sounds gloomy, but it needn't be.

Remember that you do have a tremendous freedom of choice. It's only a year, during which the world is your oyster. You can try anything from digging gardens, restaurant or bar work, milk rounds, sorting offices, busking or odd-jobbing to all kinds of community and voluntary work. The important thing is that there is enormous scope awaiting you. So explore! If you get the opportunity to travel, use it! There are organisations which promote work abroad, so ask your careers officer or enquire at the local library. If, on the other hand, you are fortunate enough to get a good job, chances are you will develop a few skills, possibly cultivate a few ideas on a future career, learn to take responsibility and make decisions in the process. The biggest advantage is having some money and maybe even being able to save some for your life ahead as a struggling student. On the negative side, you may be unlucky and not find anything productive to do – in that case, indulge your hobbies and interests, take the chance to do exactly what you've always intended to have a go at. It's a year of self-exploration as much as anything.

'But I'll forget all I learnt at school and then how will I manage?' you may wail. For some subjects, it is obviously easier to go straight on to university while you are in the right 'academic gear'.

On the other hand, many language departments like you to have a year off before coming to university so that you can travel to the countries which speak the language you are going to be studying and maybe make some contacts for when you spend your time abroad during your course (see below). Those who do this are perhaps at a slight advantage in their first year rather than at a disadvantage.

You may be worried about getting out of the habit of studying or alternatively that you'll lose the incentive to want to go back and study after a year's lapse. Let me counter your doubts by saying for a start that your university course will be nothing like your A-levels. As soon as your lecturer says 'periglaciation', 'King Lear', 'cell membranes' or 'calculus' everything clicks back into place with astonishing rapidity and you realise it wasn't forgotten in your year off. Avoid getting hooked on encyclopedia selling, getting married, being kidnapped, joining religious sects...

The biggest advantage I have found in taking time off before university (other students have said the same) is that it helps you to develop your own equipment to cope with life. If this sounds whimsical, consider the 17 or 18 year-old: straight from school, often it's the first time away from home, completely alone and being plunged into the crowded, confusing and stressful environment of a university; very often completely unable to cope. Someone a year older and wiser who has had time to grow up more, has become socially more developed and learnt to deal more effectively with totally new situations, will have the potential for settling in and getting the most out of university from the start.

... has more to say

A year abroad

All students studying modern languages (French, Spanish, German, Italian and Arabic) are required by their department to spend some time abroad. This varies according to whether you are doing a single honours course with an additional subject or a combined course comprising two languages. All single honours language students must spend a year in a country where the language they are studying is spoken and as all single honours students must do an additional subject for two years which is often, although not necessarily, a language, they must spend at least a month in the country where their additional language is spoken (this takes place in the lay vacation at the end of your first year). If you are doing combined honours you are expected to spend a year in a country where one of your languages is spoken and as much of your lay vacation in the first three years (minimum time one month) as you can, perfecting your other language in an appropriate country. Doing six months in one country then changing to another during your year abroad isn't encouraged by the language departments, because they prefer you to spend your year as an English Assistant, which is a nine-month contract – it is possible if you attend a university course in each country but it is rare.

Students generally go in their third year, except those Italian students who do not have an A-level, who must go in their second year.

Departments have lists of useful addresses and tutors are helpful with advice; however it is up to you to make arrangements if you don't want to be an English Assistant or don't get a place on the Assistantship scheme.

Several students each year can enlist on courses at foreign universities, where the workload is not usually very taxing. This has been fairly popular in the past due to the ready availability of local authority grants, although these will almost certainly be harder to get in the future.

The main drawback to this method is that these courses have a high intake of 'foreign' students (eg Brits and Americans) and it is very easy to get mixed up with them and not meet the indigenous population.

There are some lucky or some adventurous students who manage to obtain a full-time job abroad, perhaps through friends or contacts. This is much easier in EC countries where a work permit is not required. This method is highly recommended since you must cope in a demanding situation with the language and the people from the outset.

The largest group is of those students who go abroad as English Assistants to schools and colleges. These jobs are organised by the Central Bureau in London. You can generally choose where you wish to go but the occasional intervention of Sod's law means that you could be sent to the opposite end of the country. Horror stories abound of demolished schools, classes of 60 pupils, non-arrival of pay, etc, most of which are apocryphal or highly exaggerated. Pay rates vary enormously: from a pittance in Spain to extreme wealth in France (writes an envious and impoverished Hispanist) but most subsidise their pay by giving private English lessons.

However you decide to spend your year abroad, and other ways of doing it are possible with your department's permission, some problems will always arise. These can sometimes appear to be quite daunting, but almost all students come back to England having learnt and achieved a great deal; indeed, for many it is their most memorable experience at university.

6 • MONEY MATTERS

How to pay for your year off

If you've been supported or part-supported by your parents when taking A-levels or a degree or diploma course, you could be very lucky and continue this fine arrangement. Some students do: they have parents who are able and willing to finance a further period of non-earning. It is possible that some parents are glad to pay up, in order to encourage their son or daughter to go off for a year to exotic further climes – indeed the further the better.

But for most students, it's a case of 'find the money'. But where?

Local authorities

If you have already taken a degree or HND course, you will have received financial support already from your local education authority. It may be that the LEA paid fees only; your parents' income was such that you didn't qualify for a maintenance grant.

Whatever the arrangement, it's very unlikely that the LEA will support you with a grant or award for a year off. On the other hand, local authorities in the UK often do assist with travel and subsistence grants for approved study-visits. In order to win one, students need to apply to their local authority, giving details of the proposed visit and its relationship to the proposed later course, or the one just completed. *Student Grants and Loans* is a publication that explains the system of higher education grants available from LEAs – it gives details of what the grant covers, who is eligible, how to apply and when; it is available from your own LEA office or college or school, or by writing to the DFE, Sanctuary Buildings, Great Smith Street, Westminster SW1P 3BT (telephone: 071-925 5000).

Grant-givers

There are other sources of finance and publications that describe them. Among them are the following:

The British Council (established 1934) is a partially government-funded organisation that promotes British interests, culture and language abroad. The Council has offices, libraries and English teaching schools in 90 countries worldwide and is especially active in the Commonwealth countries.

Duties undertaken by the Council include the recruitment of English teachers, the provision of grants to postgraduates and foreign students wishing to study in the UK, and the provision of information on study opportunities abroad. Further information is available from The British Council, Educational Information Service, 10 Spring Gardens, London SW1A 2BN (telephone: 071-389 4383). It has to be said that most grants are for postgraduates, and it is necessary to secure a place at an institution abroad.

The Grants Register lists scholarships and research grants for UK students. It includes grants and awards at overseas universities and colleges. It also lists exchange opportunities, competitions, prizes, vocational awards and grants for students in financial difficulty. Published by Macmillan, Little Essex Street, London WC2B 4LF (telephone: 071-836 6633).

Study Abroad lists over 200,000 scholarships, awards and prizes at university level throughout the world. Published by UNESCO, 7 Place de Fontenoy, 75700 Paris, France, or from HMSO, through bookshops.

Higher Education in the European Community lists grants for students who wish to study in European Community countries. Published by Kogan Page, 120 Pentonville Road, London N1 9JN (telephone: 071-278 0433). Price £13.95.

Charities Digest lists education charities that give grants to needy students. Published by the Family Welfare Association, 501–505 Kingsland Road, London E8 4AU (telephone: 071-254 6251).

The Which? Guide to Sponsorship in Higher Education lists over 100 companies that provide sponsorships for students, for research and for industrial training. Published by the Consumers' Association, 2 Marylebone Road, London NW1 4LD, it is obtainable from bookshops.

Sponsorship and Training Opportunities in Engineering details sponsorships and training offered to sixth-form or college students applying for university engineering degree courses and for final year engineering degree students seeking a graduate training post. Available from the Institution of Mechanical Engineers, PO Box 23, Northgate Avenue, Bury St Edmunds IP32 6BN (telephone: 0284 763277).

Directory of Grant-Making Trusts is a list of voluntary grant-making bodies in England and Wales covering all fields of voluntary activities including medicine and health, welfare, education, the sciences and humanities, religion and the environment. Published by Charities Aid Foundation, 48 Pembury Road, Tonbridge, Kent TN9 2JD (telephone: 0732 771333).

Grants from Europe/How to Get Money and Influence Policy lists the funds that are available from the EC, how to assess and improve the chances of funding, and how to apply for grants. Published by NCVO Publications, Regent's Wharf, 8 All Saints Street, London N1 9RL.

European funds for travel and study

Some European Community schemes aim to assist student mobility and co-operation in higher education. Financial support is available for those participating in the schemes, for example ERASMUS (European Community Action Scheme for the Mobility of University Students), to help meet the additional costs incurred, including travel, higher costs of living and appropriate language courses. To find out about ERASMUS schemes, students should contact staff at their own college or school.

TEMPUS (Trans-European Mobility Scheme for University Studies) offers financial support in three categories: joint European projects which link enterprises and/or universities in central/eastern European countries with partners in at least two EC countries; mobility grants for higher education staff; and some other grants, including support for youth exchanges. TEMPUS operates in the following countries: Albania, Bulgaria, Estonia, Czech and Slovak Republics, Hungary, Latvia, Lithuania, Poland, Romania and Slovenia. Further information is available from the Europe Unit of the British Council at Medlock Street, Manchester M15 4AA (telephone: 061-957 7000) or from the EC TEMPUS Office, rue Montoyer 4, B–1040 Brussels, Belgium (telephone: 010 32 2 504 0711).

The Lingua programme is to distribute £130 million over five years to fund language teaching and learning projects in the EC. Lingua provides support for many projects, including language learning in small and medium-sized enterprises and aid to enable students in professional, technical and vocational education to spend time improving foreign language skills in another EC country. Information from UK Lingua Unit at the Central Bureau, Seymour Mews, London W1H 9PE (telephone: 071-224 1477).

Most students and 'year off-ers' have no grant, award, prize or 'contribution'. They use their own initiative. As students, they have become used to living on their wits, earning and spending as they go.

Use your own initiative

As you will see as you read the entries in 'Voluntary Service' and other sections of this book, volunteers are often paid travel expenses and are given pocket money. Au pairs work for wages, plus board and lodging. EFL teachers work for a wage. Students who work at summer and other vacation jobs work for wages too. The various publications that are recommended by us give information (as far as it is possible) about the financial arrangements. These publications are:

Working Holidays published by the Central Bureau for Educational Visits and Exchanges, Seymour Mews, London W1H 9PE.

Study Holidays, advice on European language courses, with details of accommodation, travel, bursaries, grants and scholarships. Also published by the Central Bureau.

Work Your Way Around the World, Summer Jobs Abroad and *Adventure Holidays* all contain information about finance as well as lists of jobs and other opportunities. Published by Vacation Work, 9 Park End Street, Oxford OX1 1HJ.

7 • SUMMER AND VACATION JOBS

A 'year off' can, of course, be shorter than a year. Most students look for a summer vacation job only; some extend this into a longer period of up to a year. Either way, a summer or a longer job can bring many of the same advantages – income, experience, the opportunity to travel and meet people.

Summer jobs are not restricted to fruit-picking and guiding saucer-eyed tourists. Jobs are available at work-camps, holiday centres, pubs, shops and hotels, and in all forms of employment where cover for staff on holiday is required.

One way to approach job-hunting is to sign up with employment agencies, who will find you a job for a fee or commission: they handle secretarial, office, warehouse and shop jobs. Or you can apply to the local council for work at leisure centres, social centres, parks or play schemes. Local newspapers are another useful source of help: they display adverts of all kinds, and they provide news of local events, which may open up the possibility of occasional work. Summer and other vacation jobs that can stretch into a 'year off' can be categorised.

Holidays

Holiday companies such as Butlins are one of the largest of the seasonal employers. They need bar staff, cleaners, waiting staff, clerical help and games organisers. The camps and holiday centres are mainly in the UK, although there are also centres in Europe. The season is long – from May to October – and helpers can be employed for the full period.

Other seasonal jobs are at mountain, sea and river holiday centres, and at safari or animal parks. Sports instructors and teachers are in special demand here, so there are plenty of opportunities for people with professional training and qualifications in swimming, archery, tennis, fell-walking, rock-climbing, windsurfing, etc. For trekking schools, knowledge of horses is obviously needed; neither do sailing schools employ amateurs.

Amusement parks and tourist resorts provide pickings, although not often rich pickings. Theme parks, tourist centres and stately homes need café, bar and security staff.

Hotels Hotels and cafés in tourist resorts by the sea or inland need summer staff too. The work is often tiring and not well paid, and unsociable hours are to be expected if you intend to work at a counter, a bar or in the restaurant.

Children Some students put 'working with children' as a priority, or option for a job. Others shudder at the thought. If you are in the first category, there are jobs at nurseries, on play schemes and camps, as au pairs or at family centres. No special qualifications are generally required, but you will certainly need energy and patience.

Organisations that are responsible for adventure holidays and play schemes for disadvantaged or disabled children often need volunteers, particularly during the summer. These may include local councils in need of leaders and instructors. Nurses are in great demand, as are trainee teachers.

The work involves creative play, the organisation of activities, including crafts and performing arts, and some domestic work. It can be emotionally and physically exhausting, and volunteers should have a good sense of humour, stamina and a willingness to work very hard. The age range looked for is generally 17 plus.

Children's summer camps, involving holiday activities with skill training in sports and games, are very popular and are expanding: they need large numbers of instructors and supervisors.

The work is not particularly well paid, but food and accommodation are generally provided free of charge, and the job can be a lot of fun (or not, depending on the centre, the children – and their parents!).

There are specialist agencies for au pairs, nannies, children's nurses and mothers' helps. Most of them advertise in the magazine *The Lady*.

Business world

Office jobs come in many shapes – typing, word-processing, clerical duties, computing – often all under the title of 'temp'. These are not restricted to girls. To find out about them, you need to find a 'temp agency' in your town (there is bound to be more than one). Employers look for real skills – good typing and shorthand speeds and knowledge of WP software packages. It can be a good idea to prepare for this kind of employment by taking a short typing and/or WP course in the evening or during the day, prior to job-hunting.

Telephone sales is much despised, but there are openings available, and students can be very good at it – or at least those with verbal dexterity and quick wits can be good at it.

The retail trade – shops – look for summer and vacation help. The large city department stores, Boots, Comet, Tesco, etc, usually need staff, although the work may be manual – shelf-filling and warehouse-stacking. The major stores do not take just anyone – you need to demonstrate interest in the retail industry and some knowledge of it.

Among other opportunities are jobs in building and construction, although they are far fewer than in previous times. Most jobs are found by asking at sites; the work is menial and heavy. There are likely to be more jobs at factories that specialise in food processing, where staff holidays take their toll. Packers, warehouse staff, delivery drivers and line workers are often required.

Language schools

Students who have a keen interest in languages can often find places teaching English as a foreign language (EFL) at schools for overseas students. These schools are often in very nice places, too – Cambridge, Oxford, London, Brighton, Edinburgh.

Another language field is teaching English abroad, in English language schools. Places can be even nicer – Madrid, Barcelona, Rome, Nice, Paris, etc. For these jobs, the 'year off' is likely to be end-on to a degree course, because the language schools look for graduates, teachers or teacher-training students.

Language schools in the UK also take on non-language teaching staff for kitchens, for the supervision of day trips and in residential centres. Occasionally there are openings for sports instructors at these schools.

On the land

As in the building trade, farm jobs are fewer than they were some years ago. However, there are still some menial summer jobs as pickers and packers on fruit farms. Pay is usually based on 'piece' rates, which means you earn in relation to the crop that is picked, or hours worked.

Voluntary work

There are complete sections of this book on voluntary work in the UK and overseas. It is a major source of employment for students. Board and lodging is generally free, but pay is low or non-existent.

Vacation jobs

The following lists may give you 'start-up' ideas for contacts that could lead to jobs. You can telephone or write to see if jobs are available.

However, a far wider range of jobs will be notified on the vacancies boards at employment offices in your area. You should call in (armed with a pad and pen) to list the firms and the vacancies. Employment offices – public and private – often carry information about jobs in other parts of the UK and overseas.

Most of the jobs that are of possible interest to you will be temporary. This may be all you are looking for, but they could also lead to jobs that last for up to a year.

PGL Young Adventure Ltd, 839 Alton Court, Penyard Lane, Ross-on-Wye, Herefordshire HR9 5NR (telephone: 0989 767833).
Staff are recruited to work at residential activity centres in the UK and in France. There are vacancies for outdoor activity instructors, for group leaders (responsible for the organisation and welfare of the children) and for various 'support' roles. The latter include kitchen staff, drivers, nurses, maintenance and domestic staff.

Working with children and students

EF Language Travel, EF House, 1–3 Farman Street, Hove, Sussex BN3 1AL (telephone: 0273 723651).
Course directors, course leaders and teachers required for English language tuition for French, Spanish and Italian children in London and south-east centres. Wages by arrangement, six days a week. Previous experience is required.

Freetime Summer Camps, Park House, Moor Lane, Woking, Surrey GU22 9RB (telephone: 0483 740242).
Activity holidays organised for children aged 4 to 15 at day centres in Surrey. Sports instructors and counsellors are needed from £70 upwards per week for a five- to seven-day week. Activities include archery, arts and crafts, canoeing, rifle shooting, tennis and windsurfing;

July–August.

HF Holidays Ltd, Redhills, Skirsgill Park, Penrith, Cumbria CA11 0DT (telephone: 0768 67670).
Children's activities organised; group leaders needed, at £46 per week plus free board and lodging. Leaders are required for July–August months at several UK locations.

Ardmore Adventure Ltd, 11–15 High Street, Marlow, Buckinghamshire SL7 1AU (telephone: 0628 890060).
Leaders and supervisors needed for adventure residential camps for 5 to 16 year-olds, located throughout the UK. Board and lodging, plus wages from £45 per week, depending on hours worked.

Camp Beaumont, 9 West Street, Godmanchester, Cambridgeshire PE18 8HG.
Residential camps need group leaders at £50 per week to plan, organise and supervise children's activities. Experience needed. Free board and lodging provided. Monitors required to supervise transportation of children and at the camps.

Holiday centres

Action Holidays Ltd, Bexton Lane, Knutsford, Cheshire WA16 9BP (telephone: 0565 654775).
About 200 staff are needed to run multi-activity centres for children aged 5 to 15 in the London area, Hampshire, Cheshire and Staffordshire. Supervisors are responsible for co-ordinating children's care; instructors are also needed for a wide range of sports activities.

Bourne Leisure Services Ltd, 51–55 Bridge Street, Hemel Hempstead, Hertfordshire HP1 1LX (telephone: 0442 69257).

This company organises over 20 holiday parks in the UK. Receptionists, bar staff, sales staff, lifeguards, site workers and children's 'aunties and uncles' are needed;

minimum age 18.

Countrywide Holidays Association, Birch Heys, Cromwell Range, Manchester M14 6HU (telephone: 061-225 1000). General assistants at a weekly rate, plus free board and lodging. Duties include domestic work. No experience is necessary.

Haven Holidays, Swan Court, Waterhouse Street, Hemel Hempstead, Hertfordshire HP1 1DS (telephone: 0442 230300).

Warner Holidays Ltd, 1 Port Way, Port Solent, Portsmouth, Hampshire PO6 4TY (telephone: 0705 478888). Holiday centres throughout the UK require chefs, catering and bar staff, cleaners, receptionists, waiting staff and nursery supervisors. Minimum wage, board and lodging.

Friendly Hotels plc, Premier House, 10 Greycoat Place, London SW1P 1SB (telephone: 071-222 8866). Waiting staff; room cleaners; bar staff; stewards. To work a 39-hour, five-day week; minimum age is 18. Board and lodging is often available.

Hotels and catering

Little Chef, Cartel Business Centre, Unit 2, Stroudley Road, Basingstoke, Hampshire RG24 0FW (telephone: 0256 812828). Catering assistants needed for catering establishments throughout the UK. Shift work; seven days a week; minimum age is 16; no experience necessary. Accommodation is not provided.

McDonald's, Contact the local restaurant.

Pizza Hut Ltd, Staff needed for kitchens, cleaning, driving. Contact the local restaurant.

Welcome Break (part of Forte Group), Newport Pagnell Service Area, M1 Motorway, Newport Pagnell, Buckinghamshire MK16 8DS (telephone: 0908 211255).

Catering, shop and forecourt staff needed at centres throughout the UK.

Factory work

Christian Salvesen Ltd, Contact local centre, listed in telephone directory, for jobs as factory production workers. Also try local temp agencies.

Outdoors and sport

Sportsmark Ltd, Sportsmark House, Ealing Road, Brentford, Middlesex TW8 0LH (telephone: 081-560 2010). Sportsground staff (mainly in southern England), drivers and supervisors. Duties include marking out courts at sports centres.

YHA, Trevelyan House, 8 St Stephen's Hill, St Albans, Hertfordshire AL1 2DY (telephone: 0727 55215). Instructors needed for YHA activity holidays; leaders for walking tours; water sports; hill crafts, etc, at many centres throughout England and Wales. Free board and lodging, plus a small weekly payment.

Language schools

Contact these organisations (addresses listed above) for EFL teachers at children's camps and language schools.

- PGL Young Adventure Ltd
- EF Language Travel
- Camp Beaumont

Other language centres requiring teachers of EFL at summer language schools are:

Anglo-World, 8 Queen's Road, London NW4 2TH (telephone: 081-202 4361).

Euro-Academy Ltd, 77a George Street, Croydon CR0 1LD (telephone: 081-681 2905).

Elizabeth Johnson Organisation, West House, West Street, Haslemere, Surrey GU27 2AE (telephone: 0428 652751).

International Study, The Manor, Hazleton, Cheltenham, Gloucestershire GL54 4EB (telephone: 0451 860379).

International Community School, 4 York Terrace East, Regents Park, London NW1 4PT (telephone: 071-935 1206).

International College, 9 Palace Gate, London W8 5LS (telephone: 071-581 9485).

Nord-Anglia Ltd, Broome House, 10 Eden Place, Cheadle, Stockport, Cheshire (telephone: 061-491 4191).

Padworth College, Reading, Berkshire RG7 4NR (telephone: 0734 833963).

Regent School, 19–23 Oxford Street, London W1R 1RF (telephone: 071-734 7455).

Tjaereborg School of English, Borough Chambers, Firvale Road, Bournemouth BH1 2JJ (telephone: 0202 556888).

Victoria School of English, 28 Graham Terrace, Sloane Square, London SW1 (telephone: 071-730 1333).

8 • A YEAR OFF
IN BRITAIN

A year off in the UK can be a worthwhile experience. It gives students a chance to reflect, to meet other people, to earn some money, to learn new skills and perhaps to make a contribution to the community by helping people or through conservation work.

In this book an outline of the job opportunities is given, with details of age, contact points, experience needed and so on. The books listed throughout offer further help to students looking for jobs. Otherwise local or national newspapers or personal contacts through friends can often lead to jobs.

The main categories of jobs in this section are as follows:

Voluntary service

A period of voluntary work in the community can be of social and educational value. Among the projects available to volunteers are: helping the inner city homeless, working in centres for ex-drug addicts or alcoholics, nursing the elderly or handicapped, and working with immigrant communities. Volunteers usually receive board and lodging and may also be given pocket money and travelling expenses. The age limits are 16 to 30 for most of these jobs.

Workcamps

These bring together a variety of skills, talents and experiences from people of different nations. Volunteers provide a service to others and become aware of their responsibility to the society in which they live and work. Workcamps generally run for periods of two to six weeks,

April–October and at other times throughout the year. The work can include building, gardening and decorating, and can also include community or conservation projects. The age range is 16 plus.

Farm work
Fruit-picking and general farm work is available from May to October. Work is also available on community and alternative farming projects; that is, helping organic farmers or working on city farms or in community gardens. Fruit-picking can be physically exhausting and is often paid at piece work rates; poor weather can affect the amount of work available. Ages mostly 17–30; families are often welcome.

Conservation work
Opportunities exist to contribute in a useful and helpful way to the environment, which includes protecting animals and plants, maintaining forest trails and bridleways, and restoring industrial heritage monuments, churches and castles. Basic board, lodging and self-catering facilities are usually provided. The work may require manual strength and it is necessary to be fit and healthy. Age limit is 16 plus.

Hotels and restaurants
Vacancies exist for chambermaids, porters, housekeepers, cooks, chefs, catering assistants, waiting staff and cleaners in hotels, restaurants and holiday centres. Accommodation is often provided, and the work is available almost all year round. Age range is 17 plus.

Archaeology
A wide range of opportunities exist for students to assist in the excavation of Britain's past, including work on prehistoric, Anglo-Saxon and Roman sites. Often, no experience is necessary as training is provided, but volunteers (who should be 16 plus) must be prepared for physical work outdoors.

Au pair posts are usually open to women aged 17–27, and are for a minimum of six months. Positions also exist for mothers' helps and nannies, and in a variety of other jobs involving working with children.

Au pair/ childcare

There are openings to teach English in language summer schools and on American-style summer camps. Applicants should be language graduates or have TEFL (Teaching English as a Foreign Language) training or experience. Teachers are often expected to take part in leisure activities and excursions. Age range is generally 20 plus.

Language teachers

Opportunities for school-leavers to do voluntary work overseas are becoming more limited. However, there are plenty of opportunities for long-term as well as short-term service to the community in this country. Of all the organisations which are included in this section, Community Service Volunteers is the biggest and turns away no prospective volunteers who meet their criteria.

Camphill Village Trust

Contact Ann Harris, Secretary, Camphill Village Trust, Delrow House, Hilfield Lane, Aldenham, Watford, Hertfordshire WD2 8DJ (telephone: 0923 856006).

Necessary qualifications Volunteers should be at least 20.

Type of service The Trust aims to help mentally handicapped people towards independence and adjustment within the security of a community. Volunteers live communally with the residents and the more permanent co-workers. The Trust runs three villages where the residents work on the land or in workshops, two town homes and a college/assessment centre.

Minimum length of service Six months, but preferably one year.

Applications No closing date.

Annual recruitment Not known.

Accommodation Board, lodging and pocket money are provided.

The Commonwealth Institute

Contact The Education Department, 230 Kensington High Street, London W8 6NQ (telephone: 071-603 4535).

Type of service Voluntary work on educational programmes.

Contact Community Service Volunteers, 237 Pentonville Road, London N1 9NJ (telephone: 071-278 6601).

Community Service Volunteers (CSV) invites all young people aged 16–35 to experience the challenge, excitement and reward of helping people in need. Every year 2,000 volunteers work throughout the UK with elderly people, adults with disabilities, children who are handicapped, in care or in trouble, and homeless people.

Volunteers work hard, have fun and gain valuable experience. You are needed to work away from home, full-time, from four to twelve months. You will receive full board, lodging and a weekly allowance. Two references are taken up and every volunteer is individually interviewed to agree their placement. Applications are welcome throughout the year.

Community Service Volunteers

Contact The Centre Director, Corrymeela Community, 5 Drumaroan Road, Ballycastle, County Antrim, Northern Ireland (telephone: 02657 62626).

Necessary qualifications A team of ten volunteers are recruited each year. A balance is sought of young adults from Ireland and overseas who are willing to live in a demanding community setting, and are able to relate to a wide range of people from different backgrounds. The Community seeks people who can handle responsibility and are willing to be flexible. Applicants who have an active Christian commitment to the work of reconciliation are preferred. Age 20–30.

Type of service Volunteers on the 'Serve and Learn' programme work at the Community's centre on the North Antrim coast at Ballycastle. They undertake domestic and manual work in running the centre as well as being directly involved with the wide variety of groups which use the centre. Corrymeela is an ecumenical community committed to the work of reconciliation, in Ireland and beyond.

The Corrymeela Community

Minimum length of service (a) As helpers in summer programmes – three weeks; (b) as long-term volunteers – 12 months beginning in September.

Applications Closing date is end of February.

Annual recruitment Ten.

Accommodation and pay Volunteers receive free accommodation, food and pocket money.

Girl Guides Association

Contact The Personnel Officer, Girl Guides Association, 17–19 Buckingham Palace Road, London SW1W 0PT (telephone: 071-834 6242).

Necessary qualifications Volunteers should hold membership of the Girl Guide movement and be aged 18 and over.

Type of service This may include administrative and domestic duties in connection with Guide houses both in the United Kingdom and abroad.

Minimum length of service One month. Very few vacancies.

Applications Should be made as far in advance as possible.

Accommodation and pay Dependent on type and place of project. Travel fares are paid by the volunteer.

Glasgow Simon Community

Contact The Support Group, Glasgow Simon Community, 133 Hill Street, Garnethill, Glasgow G3 6UB (telephone: 041-332 3448).

Necessary qualifications Volunteers must be 18 years or over. Attitudes are important; the Community aims to accept people as they are, to live with them on an equal basis without patronising them. The work is demanding, so emotional stability and reasonable physical fitness are necessary.

Type of service Volunteers contact and offer friendship and practical help to men and women who have been homeless for a long time, especially those who sleep rough. They live in small group homes with ex-homeless people, sharing in group living, giving and receiving support, and taking responsibility for money and medicines.

Minimum length of service Six months, preferably longer.

Applications Accepted at any time of the year.

Annual recruitment Average 18.

Accommodation and pay Volunteers receive full board and lodging (with separate accommodation for days off), a weekly personal allowance, an allowance for a holiday every three months, and travel expenses. (Please note legislation passed in April 1993 may affect the accuracy of this entry.)

Contact Volunteers' Secretary, 90–92 Bromham Road, Bedford, Bedfordshire MK40 2QH (telephone: 0234 350853).

Homes for Homeless People

Founded 1970. The object is to work on behalf of single homeless people.

Necessary qualifications Volunteers must be 18 years or over.

Type of service Activities include the establishment of independent Cyrenian and other groups who organise residential community houses and make some form of basic provision for those who would otherwise sleep rough. These projects are staffed by small teams of volunteer workers who share their lives with the residents for periods of 6–12 months.

Annual recruitment Approximately 300 in any one year.

Pay Details on application to the Volunteers' Secretary.

L'Arche Ltd, 14 London Road, Beccles, Suffolk NR34 9NH (telephone: 0502 715329).

L'Arche

L'Arche communities are places where people with learning difficulties work together in a simple way. Volunteers are needed to work in a community with people with a mental handicap. The organisation views the spiritual life of working together as being as important as material welfare.

Assistants need to be at least 18. Craft skills are useful for workshops and for domestic duties. Free board and lodging are provided, plus pocket money of around £20 a week.

Most communities ask volunteers to stay for six months, but one year is preferable. Many assistants stay on for between one and two years.

From mid-1993 the address of L'Arche will be 10 Briggate, Silsden, Keighley, West Yorkshire BD20 9JT. For further information send an sae for a booklet.

The Leonard Cheshire Foundation

Contact Secretary to the Personnel Adviser, The Leonard Cheshire Foundation, 26–29 Maunsel Street, London SW1P 2QN. Telephone 071-828 1822 for details of Voluntary Work Scheme and application form.

Necessary qualifications Volunteers should be over 18 years of age, and have a genuine concern for the disabled. Previous experience is an advantage, but not essential. Good knowledge of English language and communication skills are needed.

Type of service Mainly helping with the care of severely physically handicapped residents.

Minimum length of service Two months, but few vacancies are for less than three months.

Applications Immediate vacancies are rare, so allow as long as possible. Please state dates you can offer, and duration of service.

Annual recruitment 70–80.

Accommodation and pay Board and accommodation (sometimes sharing) provided in a home, with pocket money (£25 per week, reviewed each year). Travel expenses paid by volunteer.

Contact The Personnel Officer, The Ockenden Venture, Ockenden, Constitution Hill, Woking, Surrey GU22 7UU (telephone: 0483 772012). Write with age and whether you have a driving licence, work experience, and state any special skills and interests.

The Ockenden Venture

Necessary qualifications Volunteers should be over 18.

Minimum length of service One year.

Applications Can be made at any time, but the main intake of staff takes place in August and September. In May the organisation looks for two or three summer holiday helpers.

Annual recruitment Approximately 12–18.

Accommodation and pay Board and accommodation are provided. Volunteers receive pocket money of £22 minimum per week.

Serves the sick and disabled of all age groups. Most volunteers work at the Sue Ryder Home and Head-quarters, Cavendish, Suffolk and at other Sue Ryder Homes.

The Sue Ryder Foundation

Contact Further information and application forms are available from: Sue Ryder Foundation Headquarters, Cavendish, Sudbury, Suffolk CO10 8AY (telephone: 0787 280252).

Type of service Volunteers work alongside staff, doing whatever work is necessary such as helping with the patients, domestic, office or other work. The allocation of work has to be decided on the basis of priorities arising. Volunteers need to be flexible and adaptable and have a strong sense of responsibility and dedication.

Accommodation and pay Free meals and simple accommodation are provided plus pocket money.

The normal minimum period of service is two months, although at times it may be possible to consider shorter periods. Volunteers are particularly needed in the months September to June. Early application is essential for the months of July and August. Applicants must be aged at least 16 plus.

SHAD **Support and Housing Assistance for People with Disabilities**
Contact Karen Osborn, Support Worker, SHAD Wandsworth, The Nightingale Centre, 8 Balham Hill, London SW12 9EA (telephone: 081-675 6095).
Necessary qualifications None.
Type of service SHAD recruits full-time volunteers throughout the year, to act as 'the arms and legs' of severely physically disabled people. Volunteers provide 24-hour cover, working shifts (usually one day on, two days off), and work on a one-to-one basis with disabled tenants, thus enabling them to live independently in their own homes around south-west London. Accommodation and a weekly allowance are provided. Excellent work experience in a friendly and supportive atmosphere.
Minimum length of service Four months (no upper limit).
Annual recruitment Approx 80 placements.
Accommodation and pay Free accommodation, food allowance and pocket money and travel expenses.

Shaftesbury Society
Help is needed at the Shaftesbury Holiday Centre in Essex; the guests are elderly, physically handicapped and have some medical problems. Helpers should be sympathetic towards the Christian aims and principles of the Society.
The Society looks for unpaid helpers of 16 plus for one or two weeks although travelling expenses can be claimed. Free board and lodging.
Contact Mrs Pat Ford, Volunteers' Secretary, The Shaftesbury Society Holiday Centre, New Hall, Low Road, Dovercourt, Harwich, Essex CO12 3TS (telephone: 0255 504219).

Contact The Director, Voluntary Service Belfast, 70–72 Lisburn Road, Belfast, Northern Ireland BT9 6AF (telephone: Belfast (0232) 329499).

Voluntary Service Belfast

Necessary qualifications Applicants must be over 16.

Type of service VSB is the volunteer bureau for the city of Belfast and arranges voluntary work opportunities on its own project and with other agencies. This involves work with the elderly, disabled, children, and young people. The work includes conservation, decorating, visiting, clerical and crime prevention.

Annual recruitment Open.

Information about voluntary work opportunities in the Greater London area is available from local volunteer bureaux, which can be found in the London telephone directory under Voluntary Work Information Service – Local Advisory Services. In case of difficulty, contact 444 Brixton Road, London SW9 8EJ (telephone: 071-274 4000).

London

The Scottish Community Education Council, West Coartes House, 90 Haymarket Terrace, Edinburgh EH12 5LQ (telephone: 031-313 2488). Promotes community involvement and service by young people in Scotland. It provides an information and advisory service and refers volunteers to appropriate organisations and schemes. It issues information sheets, newsletters, directories of summer opportunities, and pamphlets on helping with children, the elderly and the handicapped and on other aspects of voluntary work in Scotland.

Scotland

Information and Research Manager, Wales Council for Voluntary Action, Lys Ifor, Crescent Road, Caerffili, Mid Glamorgan CF8 1XL (telephone: Caerffili (0222) 869224). Provides information about voluntary work opportunities in Wales – see *A Short Guide to Voluntary*

Wales

Work Opportunities in Wales. WCVA Information sheet no 3.

Ireland

See *Og Irish Youth Handbook* (cost of postage only), published by the National Youth Council of Ireland, 3 Montague Street, Dublin 2 (telephone: Dublin (010 353 1) 784122).

Further information

The National Youth Agency, 17–23 Albion Street, Leicester LE1 6GD (telephone: 0533 471200). Can provide information about community involvement opportunities for young people in England and Wales. Three information sheets are available, giving useful contacts: *Voluntary Work Abroad, Voluntary Work Placements* and *Voluntary Work and Young People*. Each costs 50p plus postage and packing.

Volunteer bureaux There are more than 300 volunteer bureaux throughout the UK. Bureaux are 'job shops' for volunteers, and provide information about a wide range of local opportunities. They give advice and guidance on how prospective volunteers can use their time, and they find people specific jobs to do by referring them to a statutory agency (for instance, a social services department), voluntary organisation or informal volunteer group. Some bureaux also recruit volunteers for projects they have initiated themselves. Check out your local volunteer bureau by looking in the telephone directory under Volunteer Bureaux or Council for Voluntary Service, or call at your Citizens' Advice Bureau or town hall information desk.

If there isn't a volunteer bureau in your town, then you might be interested in starting one. The National Association of Volunteer Bureaux will be happy to advise you on how to go about it. Please write to The National Association of Volunteer Bureaux, St Peter's College,

College Road, Saltley, Birmingham B8 3TE (telephone: 021-327 0265).

An essential book on voluntary work is *The International Directory of Voluntary Work*, £8.95 plus 75p for postage and packing, published by Vacation Work, 9 Park End Street, Oxford OX1 1HJ.

8 B • WORKCAMPS AND SUMMER PROJECTS

A different form of voluntary service, particularly useful for students with only short periods to spare, is available at workcamps. Workcamps are usually held during the summer and last from two to four weeks. The work varies from camp to camp but is generally unskilled or semiskilled. Volunteers could be involved in manual work (decorating, building, setting up adventure playgrounds), running holiday schemes for old or handicapped people, or fruit-picking. They are expected to work hard for about 35–40 hours a week and to take a full part in the social life of the camp. Free board and accommodation are usually given, but volunteers pay their own travel fares and receive no pay. A registration fee is often required.

Acorn Projects (The National Trust) PO Box 12, Westbury, Wiltshire BA13 4NA (telephone: 0373 826826). Runs a series of more than 330 voluntary work projects in England and Wales from March until November. The work usually consists of outdoor conservation schemes on the Trust's many beautiful properties, often in remote places. There are occasional indoor tasks, and the volunteers sometimes stay in the Trust's historic houses, otherwise in buildings such as hostels, schools and village halls.

Each project lasts a week and is composed of about 12 people. Volunteers pay from £35 a week towards the cost of food and accommodation.

Minimum age 16.

Closing date for applications None, but the places for women get filled very quickly.

Annual recruitment 3,000 approx.

Manor House, High Birstwith, Harrogate HG3 2LG (telephone: 0423 770385). Volunteers aged 16–30 to work at 26 cathedrals helping with conservation, restoration and maintenance. Camp duration one week. Cost per week £33. Last week in July to first week in September.

Cathedral Camps

The Corrymeela Community
See page 103.

Friends House, 173–177 Euston Road, London NW1 2BJ (telephone: 071-387 3601). QISP organises voluntary projects in the United Kingdom. The projects (which usually run for one to three weeks) involve a group of volunteers, half from abroad, who live and work together to help meet a need in the local community. There is a variety of project work to choose from each year, for instance manual work, work in hospitals or with children. The projects are enjoyable and offer a chance to get away and meet others and gain new skills. Volunteers must pay their own travel costs but the food and accommodation during the project are free. The lower age limit for applications is 18 years.

Quaker International Social Projects (QISP)

Closing date for applications None, although most projects are full by mid-June. It is worth applying for last-minute places. The final summer programme is published in April. Application is by form supplied and a registration fee is payable.

Contact Reserves Management Department, The Lodge, Sandy, Bedfordshire SG19 2DL (telephone: 0767 680551).
Has places for voluntary wardens on RSPB nature reserves in Britain, assisting the permanent warden, carrying out physical reserve management work, such as clearing ponds or building paths, helping with visitors and carrying out surveys. An interest in and some

The Royal Society for the Protection of Birds (RSPB)

knowledge of birds is an advantage. Accommodation is free, but volunteers pay their own transport to and from the reserve and provide own food. Volunteers are required all year round.

Minimum age 16.

Toc H National Projects Co-ordinator, 1 Forest Close, Wendover, Aylesbury, Buckinghamshire HP22 6BT (telephone: 0296 623911).

Toc H runs short-term residential projects throughout the year lasting from a weekend up to three weeks. Most of these are in Britain and include working with disabled people, children in need, on playschemes and camps, and on conservation projects. Toc H also runs projects in Germany where volunteers work with the families of British service personnel (see page 167).

Further details in the Toc H Projects Programme, published twice yearly on the first Monday of March and September.

Minimum age 16 (18 for some projects). No maximum.

Eligibility EC citizens are given preference.

Closing date for applications None but early application is advised.

Annual recruitment 500+.

Further information *Working Holidays* is published annually by the Central Bureau, Seymour Mews, London W1H 9PE (telephone: 071-486 5101). 1993 edition £7.95 (plus £1.50 p&p). This book devotes 47 pages to working holidays in Great Britain. Types of work include au pair work, community work, jobs with children, domestic work, farm work, work camps and vacancies for leaders and guides.

8C • CONSERVATION PROJECTS AND HOLIDAYS

The opportunities for helping out on conservation projects are substantial. The bad news is that much of the work is unpaid. It is often a voluntary activity, organised locally and dependent on goodwill. For young people looking for a cash return, it is not often worthwhile, and not many people (no matter what their age) can afford to work without pay.

On the other hand, voluntary work is good for CVs. It impresses employers to see initiative and enterprise being used to improve the quality of the environment, whether it is locally or far from home. Therefore, a long-term view may be that to spend some weeks working on a conservation project is perhaps a good move in the search for that elusive 'good job' later on.

For the information on the following organisations, the publishers acknowledge the help of the Central Bureau for Educational Visits and Exchanges: Derbyshire International Youth Camp, Ironbridge Gorge Museum, Ffestiniog Railway Company, the National Trust, Operation Osprey and The Waterway Recovery Group.

There are various kinds of voluntary (or even paid) conservation work. They fall into these categories:

1 Outdoor conservation schemes are run by the National Trust, BTCV and other organisations listed in the 'Work-camps and summer projects' section of this book. There are organisations such as the Landmark Trust, which rescues places and buildings in distress, revives them and gives them new life. For example, Lundy Island in the Bristol Channel is a Landmark project, under a lease from the National Trust.

2 Work with birds and animals is possible by volunteering at your local centres. In addition, the Royal Society for the Protection of Birds has places for voluntary workers on RSPB nature reserves throughout the UK.

RSPB, The Lodge, Sandy, Bedfordshire SG19 2DL (telephone: 0767 680551).

Animal shelters also look for voluntary help. Try local centres.

3 Indoor conservation generally means assisting with the repair and restoration of historic places. Obviously, the skills of carpentry, cementing, plastering and glazing are useful, but not normally held by young people. Volunteers are therefore pressed into use as labourers. Again, the work is generally unpaid and there may be accommodation charges. See the entry for Quaker workcamps in this book, and *Working Holidays 1993*, published by the Central Bureau, for ideas and contacts.

4 Other conservation projects These projects also look for volunteer help, sometimes with payment.

Beach Head NT C/o The Regional Office, Lanhydrock, Bodmin, Cornwall PL30 4ED (telephone: 0208 74281). Volunteers are needed to help clear litter from Cornish beaches. Each morning volunteers are taken to a beach, where they spend up to three hours collecting litter from among rocks and sand dunes. The 12-day 'holidays' (afternoons are free) in July and August cost £110. This covers all meals and accommodation at Beach Head National Trust base-camp, a converted barn on a remote part of the coast. Facilities include hot showers, drying room, common room with log fire and fully equipped kitchen. A minibus is available for outings and expeditions. Volunteers help with cleaning, preparing meals and washing-up. Participants pay their own travel expenses and should take a sleeping-bag. Enclose a large sae for further information.

The NT in Cornwall also takes on long-term volunteers. Accommodation is provided. Students should have relevant qualifications, such as degrees in biology or environmental science.

British Trust for Conservation Volunteers

BTCV, 36 St Mary's Street, Wallingford, Oxfordshire OX10 0EU (telephone: 0491 39766). BTCV runs nearly 600 Natural Break conservation working holidays throughout England, Wales and Northern Ireland. These run all year, including Christmas and New Year. Prices start at £27.50 per week and cover accommodation and food. The accommodation can vary from a basic village hall, to a volunteer centre, to a holiday cottage, and this is reflected in the price.

The practical conservation work undertaken on the projects includes coppicing, dry-stone-walling, footpath work, managing waterways and habitat management.

Volunteers must be 16 and over (upper age limit 84). No experience is required as full training will be given. You do need to be physically fit and have plenty of enthusiam.

Opportunities also exist for long-term volunteers at volunteer centres throughout the country to organise practical projects and assist with local administration. This is an ideal way to gain experience in practical conservation.

BTCV also have over 1,000 local groups working most weekends and numerous mid-week projects throughout the country. There is also an extensive programme of training courses covering various conservation skills. Other courses teach such skills as basic photography, first-aid and leadership.

To receive a Natural Break brochure, ring the brochure line on 0491 824602, or for more information on the opportunities available, write to the above address enclosing an sae.

Derbyshire International Youth Camp

Derbyshire County Council, Community Education Department, County Offices, Matlock, Derbyshire DE4 3AG (telephone: 0629 580000 ext 6417).

International workcamps at Elvaston Castle Country Park and Shipley Park are intended to improve the environment and develop understanding between young people from different countries. Among the current projects are constructing woodland walks, rebuilding a footbridge, erecting fencing, improving drainage and scrub clearance, plus work on a children's adventure play area. As well as doing manual work, young people are encouraged to help on a community service project, which involves helping on play schemes. An extensive leisure programme is arranged. Ages 16–21. Training in the use of tools is given and full supervision provided at all times. One to two weeks, late July to mid-August. Five-day week.

Accommodation is provided in a residential school, with sports and recreational facilities. Everyone helps with meals and cleaning duties. The cost of £25 per week covers food and accommodation. There are 20 free places available for young Derbyshire people. Qualifies under the Duke of Edinburgh's Award Scheme. Apply by 1 May.

Earthwatch

Earthwatch has attracted the greatest interest of all. Founded in the US over 20 years ago, it opened its European office in Oxford two years ago. A non-profit-making organisation, Earthwatch's mission is to match field scientists needing money and manpower with members of the public willing to help. Its services are in great demand since scientific funding is drying up at a time when ecological problems are multiplying.

Earthwatch Europe, Belsyre Court, 57 Woodstock Road, Oxford OX2 6HU (telephone: 0865 311600). Fax 0865 311383.

Earthwatch serves as a bridge between the public and the scientific community. To date, Earthwatch has co-ordinated the involvement of over 28,000 adult men and women in research expeditions worldwide. They have contributed nearly £9 million and over 2.75 million hours of labour to earth, human and life sciences in the field. Over 1,000 scientists, in 87 countries, have been funded in the life and cultural sciences which have been assisted by Earthwatch team-members.

A funding source and a workforce in one, Earthwatch team members share the costs of mobilising the research expeditions. For two or three weeks, team members may learn to excavate, map, photograph, gather data, make collections, assist diving operations and share all other field chores associated with professional expedition re-search. They are looking for people to help and learn. No special skills are required.

Once in the field, your contribution (which varies with the nature of the project, but currently averages £700) covers all your costs, excluding travel. Students and teachers may apply for Earthwatch fellowship grants. Accommodation can range from tents to hotels, and meals are usually local dishes. Earthwatch publishes a bi-monthly magazine containing information of its 150 projects worldwide, which is available with annual mem-bership of £22 (£30 outside Europe).

Volunteer Resource Officer, Harbour Station, Porth-madog, Gwynedd LL49 9NF (telephone: 0766 512340). Volunteers are required to help in the maintenance and running of this famous narrow-gauge railway. A wide

Ffestiniog Railway Company

variety of work is possible. This can mean working in booking offices, guards' vans, buffet cars, shops, cafés and small sales outlets; cleaning locomotives; working on the footplate and driving; turning, welding, machining, steam-fitting, sheet-metal work, joinery, upholstery and paintwork. Other work includes the repair of fences, bridges, culverts and heavy walling. Volunteers also help in the museum at Porthmadog, with painting, carpentry and metalwork, helping to create new displays, and maintaining the historic buildings, parks and gardens. Training is given where necessary. Qualifies under the Duke of Edinburgh's Award Scheme. Ages 16 and over, unless in a supervised party. All volunteers must be physically fit. Limited self-catering hostel accommodation is available for regular volunteers, for which a small charge is made. Camping space and lists of local accommodation are also available.

Groundwork Trust

Formed in 1982, the growing network of Groundwork Trusts set out to bring together local people and community groups in partnerships for practical action tackling environmental problems of dereliction, to restore landscapes and to make positive use of waste land. Currently there are 31 Trusts which need help. The benefits are substantial; a new vision of a brighter future in which everyone plays a part in looking after Britain's outdoor living space.

The Groundwork Foundation, 85–87 Cornwall Street, Birmingham B3 3BY (telephone: 021-236 8565).

Ironbridge Gorge Museum Trust

The Wharfage, Ironbridge, Telford, Shropshire TF8 7AW (telephone: 0952 433522).

The Trust was established in 1967 to conserve, restore and interpret the rich industrial heritage of the Gorge, the birthplace of the Industrial Revolution. The Museum comprises six main sites and has been created around a unique series of industrial monuments, concentrated on the iron and pottery industries, and spreads over some six square miles. Volunteers are needed to work on various sites, which involves industrial archaeology, research, excavation, interpretation of exhibits and general site duties. Low-cost hostel accommodation is available on site or in a youth hostel nearby. Participants pay for their own food. Own transport, bicycle/car, is usually essential. Participants can enter Museum sites free.

Contact either the National Trust, 36 Queen Anne's Gate, London SW1H 9AS (telephone: 071-222 9251) for information on national projects (mostly done through Acorn Projects, which is described elsewhere), or The National Trust for Scotland at 5 Charlotte Square, Edinburgh EH2 4DU (telephone: 031-226 5922).

National Trust

The National Trust was founded to promote the preservation of fine buildings, beautiful landscapes and historic places. Young volunteers are needed to help with the care and preservation of the countryside and historic buildings through indoor and outdoor conservation projects, which would not otherwise be possible. Recent projects have included sand-dune stabilisation, footpath construction and repair, and erosion control. Ages 16 and over. Volunteers should be fit for hard practical work, eight-hour days, six-day weeks. One to two weeks, March–October. Similar weekend tasks are carried out by local Trust volunteer groups on NT properties in their area. An experienced leader and/or a Trust Ranger Naturalist supervises all practical work, and gives instruction in the safe use of tools. One day is free for recreation and exploration in the local area. Insurance, hostel-type or base-camp accommodation and food are provided, but volunteers help with catering arrangements and other chores. Old clothes, waterproofs, a sleeping-bag and boots or wellingtons should be taken to all camps. Qualifies under the Duke of Edinburgh's Award Scheme. Participants pay their own travel costs and contribute £35 towards food and accommodation. Volunteers completing 40 hours of voluntary work receive free access to all NT properties for one year.

Operation Osprey

The Royal Society for the Protection of Birds, Grianan, Nethy Bridge, Inverness-shire PH25 3EF (telephone: 047 983 694).

Volunteer wardens and cooks are needed at the Loch Garten Reserve in the ancient Caledonian Forest, Strathspey. Teams of volunteer wardens keep a 24-hour watch from the hide and are expected to maintain a log of the ospreys' activities, as well as spending time talking to visitors about the RSPB's work at Loch Garten. Volunteers work on a shift basis, with every third day free, and also help with camp chores. Ages 18 and over. One or more weeks between 27 March and 4 September. Full board and camping/caravan accommodation is provided at Inchdryne Farm, for a nominal charge of £15 per week. Volunteers should take a sleeping-bag, warm clothing and walking boots.

Peak Park Conservation Volunteers

Peak District National Park, National Park Office, Volunteers' Organiser, Aldern House, Baslow Road, Bakewell, Derbyshire DE45 1AE (telephone: 0629 814321).

Volunteer opportunities exist for dry-stone-walling, scrub and pond clearance, hedge-laying, footpath construction, fencing and other practical countryside work. Age group 14–65, groups on site every weekend throughout the year. Limited mid-week tasks, but working holidays available in partnership with BTCV.

Tools and insurance provided, but not food or travel costs.

Local hostels and campsites with good facilities are available, but volunteers must make their own arrangements.

In Scotland, the independent **Scottish Conservation Projects** runs weekly and fortnightly holidays from March to December costing £3 a day. SCP's Action Breaks are set up along the same lines as the Natural Breaks south of the border, though in somewhat more remote locations, and perhaps with a greater emphasis on building work.

Scottish Conservation Projects, Balallan House, 24 Allen Park, Stirling FK8 2QG (telephone: 0786 479697).

Scottish Conservation Projects

International Youth Service, Temple of Peace, Cathays Park, Cardiff CF1 3AP (telephone: 0222 223088).

United Nations (Wales)

Opportunities are available for volunteers to work in hundreds of international volunteer projects in 30 countries, in four continents. Each placement lasts two to three weeks. Volunteers must pay a fee and arrange their own transport to the project. Food, accommodation and insurance are provided. Mostly manual conservation and reconstruction work. Mostly July–August. 17 years and over. Send A5 sae for reply.

John Glock, 47 Melfort Drive, Leighton Buzzard, Bedfordshire LU7 7XN (telephone: 0525 382311).

The Waterway Recovery Group

The national co-ordinating body for voluntary labour on the inland waterways of Britain. Formed in 1970 to promote and co-ordinate local trusts and societies involved in restoring abandoned and derelict waterways to a navigable state. Volunteers are needed on summer workcamps to help with this work. There are many active projects, including excavating and laying foundations for a new canal bridge, building walls and parapets, dredging and banking, clearing vegetation, pile-driving, fitting lock gates, bricklaying and demolition work. Ages 16 and over. Parental consent is required for those under 18. Work is unpaid and mostly unskilled.

Volunteers should be fit, willing to work hard in all weathers, and able to live harmoniously in fairly close contact with the other 10–20 volunteers at each camp. One or more weeks, July–September, Christmas and Easter. Basic accommodation is provided in village halls or similar, plus three good meals a day at a charge of approximately £15 per week. Volunteers should take their own sleeping-bag and old clothes, and be prepared to help with domestic chores. Insurance is provided. Qualifies under the Duke of Edinburgh's Award Scheme. Limited places; apply by June, enclosing sae.

8 D • VACATION JOBS AND OTHER PAID WORK

There are always opportunities for vacation work and other paid temporary jobs, so long as you are prepared to take the time and trouble to look for them. Many young people find work through friends, relatives or chance contacts, which suggests that if you are looking for a job it pays to let as many people know as possible.

Quite a few students find work by careful study of the 'situations vacant' columns of the local paper or through the local Jobcentre (to be found under Employment Agencies in the *Yellow Pages*). Others find work through the local Careers Office (to be found in the telephone directory under the Education Department of your local County Council). Alternatively you may use (at no charge) the services of private employment agencies, which are useful for finding office or clerical work and, often, all sorts of manual work.

In areas of high unemployment it may be especially difficult to find a job. If it looks as if you will spend weeks fruitlessly looking for work, one solution would be to move to another part of the country to a seasonal job where accommodation is provided – work in a hotel or holiday camp, or fruit-picking on a farm, for example.

Many students derive extra benefit from temporary employment by taking a job related to their course or to the career they hope to enter after qualifying. This can be a painless and profitable way of gaining experience of a particular industry or profession at ground level, to see if you really like it. If successful, the experience will stand you in good stead later, while if it is unsuccessful you may have discovered your true bent, and when you eventually make the transition to the world of work you will find it less of a jolt. Some industries, particularly in the field of engineering, run more organised training schemes, details of which are to be found below in the section on industrial training. Most students, however, may prefer to contact local firms informally. Work in banks, laboratories, libraries and solicitors' offices, for example, has frequently been arranged with success.

Archaeological digs

Information about excavations and other archaeological fieldwork can be obtained from the Council for British Archaeology, Bowes Morrell House, York YO1 2UA (telephone: 0904 671417). Individual membership of the Council costs £15 within the UK and includes a magazine, *British Archaeological News*, published ten times a year (on the first Friday of each month with the exception of January and August) with bi-monthly supplements giving details of many projects throughout Britain. Members also automatically belong to CBA Regional Groups who can provide more detailed information on projects in their area. It is possible to subscribe to the magazine without joining the Council for £14 per year. You should then write to the director of the project in which you are interested. Some form of subsistence pay is sometimes provided; previous experience is not necessarily required.

The Army

Information about the Army Short Service Limited Commissions scheme can be obtained from the Directorate of Army Recruiting, Ministry of Defence, DAR1D, MoD, Room 1125, Empress State Building, London SW6 1TR (telephone: 071-385 1244 ext 3100). Each year about 40 young men and women waiting to go up to university are offered Short Service Limited

Commissions in the Army. They serve from four to eighteen months as officers in regular units, and have no further liability. A salary of £9,318 for 1993/94 is paid to those on the 18-month commission, together with a uniform allowance. Applicants must have reached the age of 18 years and be under 20 years on the day of commissioning, and must have already gained a university place. The closing dates for applications are 31 September for those starting in January, and 30 June for an October start.

A student who took part in the scheme wrote that it was: *'Not a recruiting effort, only a public relations exercise, ie to disseminate a sympathetic attitude to the Army in university and beyond. After only a month's very rushed training, I was in Germany and soon fulfilling a normal junior officer's job, ie administering a troop of three tanks and the crews of 11 men besides myself. Although it is not the life for me, I enjoyed the responsibility and the complete break from academic pursuits. The scheme is financially very rewarding, valuable in terms of experience, and entails no commitment to the Army during or after university.'*

Au pair/ domestic work

Domestic work may involve looking after the children or the house, working as a home help or companion, or even helping in the garden or on the farm. Many jobs are to be found by looking in newspapers or magazines, such as *The Times* or *The Lady*. For those who like horses and the outdoor life, as well as children, there are often suitable vacancies advertised in *Horse and Hound*. Work as a home help is sometimes to be found through local social services departments. And if all else fails, why not try the 'Strong healthy lad/lass seeks work, will consider anything legal' type of ad in your local newspaper?

One student worked as a private nanny for nine weeks:

'Found the job by contacting agencies who advertised in

The Lady *magazine. I quite enjoyed the job although, like many temporary nanny jobs, I seemed to spend much of my time acting as a housemaid instead. The hours were long, as I lived in, but this had the advantage that I spent very little of what I earned. I found living with people from a different social class, who had a completely different outlook on life, extremely interesting.'*

Building site work

Jobs as building labourers can be found by applying to the foreman of a local site, or by writing to one of the large construction companies, or through a Jobcentre.

One student wrote of his experience:
'I spent ten weeks working as a labourer on a building site. I met some great characters and made some good friends with other students working there. The job pays reasonably well and is usually very varied. I very rarely did the same job for more than two or three days running. For anyone who enjoys working in the open air, this is the ideal opportunity – I got a better suntan while I was working than when I went with some friends to Majorca towards the end of the holiday.'

Another student described being a building labourer as:
'The best ten weeks of my life so far.'

Factory work

Many students find that routine factory work, while often uninteresting in itself, has given them first-hand experience of industry at shop-floor level and has brought them into contact with a wider section of society.

'Even though the job (in a packing department) was far from interesting, I found the people on the factory floor very friendly.'

'It made me fully realise the deathly kind of job many people have to do.'

One student who continued to work, along with other

students, while there was a five-week unofficial strike at a canning factory, wrote:

'I was able to understand fully why industrial action was taken, and the deficiencies of the factory system.'

Manpower is one of the world's largest private work contractors, operating in 32 countries through 700 offices and directly employing some 500,000 people each year. It is not an employment agency but directly employs its staff, providing labour to various employers as needed. Work available might include industrial tasks (eg warehousing, labouring, portering, packing, etc), light assembly work (eg factory production line, packing, labelling, etc) and general office duties (eg relatively unskilled clerical work). Students would be well advised to approach their local Manpower office (see telephone directory) at the time they are available for work, as opportunities will depend on the contracts which Manpower is undertaking or is about to undertake at that time.

General

Many hospitals, especially mental and geriatric ones, are short-staffed and are pleased to receive direct enquiries from students for posts as ancillary workers. Hospitals that are in isolated positions away from towns find it particularly difficult to get staff.

Contact details for hospitals can be found in your *Yellow Pages* under Hospitals and Health Authorities and Services.

Community Service Volunteers, 237 Pentonville Road, London N1 9NJ (telephone: 071-278 6601) operates some projects involving work in hospitals. See page 103.

Hospital and nursing auxiliaries

Many firms run student apprenticeship schemes whereby the student does a year before going up to university and, in some cases, a further year after leaving. This is

Industrial training

particularly valuable for engineers, since it gives them an idea of the practical application of their theoretical work and also – if it is a 1-3-1 scheme – contributes to the period of practical experience required for professional status. In some cases the pre-university period is part of an industrial scholarship scheme, with the firm also paying the student's fees and grant while at university.

Further information

The following publications will give you information about these schemes, but many firms who do not run a formal scheme would be willing to arrange some industrial training, so it might be worthwhile writing direct to any firm you are particularly interested in. Read *The Which? Guide to Sponsorships in Higher Education*, from *Which?*, 2 Marylebone Road, London NW1 4DX.

The Careers Counsellors' Job Book, published annually for CRAC by Hobsons Publishing PLC, Bateman Street, Cambridge CB2 1LZ (telephone: 0223 354551). Gives details of training schemes offered by British employers for those entering employment, from 16 year-old school-leavers to graduates. *The Careers Counsellors' Job Book* is distributed to all secondary schools and main careers offices in England, Wales and Scotland and is intended to help careers counsellors giving advice. It also provides a guide to further and higher education opportunities.

Sponsorships, published by the Careers and Occupational Information Centre (COIC), Moorfoot, Sheffield S1 4PQ (telephone: 0742 704563). An annual publication, giving details of employers and professional bodies offering sponsorships and supplementary awards.

A much more detailed analysis of courses, institutions and subjects that are sponsored is provided in the *Which?* guide described above.

A number of different temporary jobs may be available with the local authority, particularly in the highways, planning, education and social services departments. Traffic census work has proved popular among students and is often available in the summer months.

Local authority work

One student who worked in a social services department for six months wrote:

'My official position was a temporary welfare assistant in one of the four area teams. The job included issuing bus passes, paying initial visits to people needing wheelchairs or admittance to old people's homes, etc. We co-ordinated with bodies such as the Department of Social Security, the Housing Department and WRVS.'

For temporary office or secretarial work, you should contact one of the private employment agencies or staff bureaux listed in the *Yellow Pages*. The high street agencies include Alfred Marks, Brook Street Bureau, Kelly Girl, Manpower and Reed. It is worth contacting lesser-known agencies as their rates are often very competitive. Even if you have no office skills, they may be able to find you unskilled work.

Office work

Alternatively, try the local Jobcentre. Jobcentres now have notice of temporary vacancies.

Opportunities available during the summer months include working in hotels and holiday camps, acting as leaders or guides to foreign visitors, teaching English to foreigners, acting as outdoor pursuits instructors, working in seaside towns or holiday resorts or for a local parks department. Some useful addresses are listed in the book *Working Holidays* mentioned at the end of this section. Some comments from students indicate the variety of work available:

Seasonal work

'I spent two months as a chambermaid in a London hotel. I found the job by contacting hotels listed in the British Tourist Authority's book Hotels and Restaurants in Britain. *After about two weeks the work became mechanical and deadly boring, but the hours were reasonable and allowed me to see London, which was the main purpose.'*

'I worked as a barmaid and waitress in a small hotel in Stratford-upon-Avon. I served drinks and snacks while dressed in Old English costume. I learned a lot about the hotel trade and tourists but disliked the hours and the late nights. The bar work was very interesting: meeting people and learning about drinks.'

'. . . seasonal employment for Scarborough Corporation Entertainments, working as a car-park attendant on the foreshore. It was in the open air, with easy hours, and the only mental exercise was reconciling the money with the tickets sold.'

'My father heard from the head of the Parks department that they employed people (students mainly) for the summer months. I was employed primarily as a weed-sprayer but that involved only two months of my time. For the most part I did the usual gardening jobs, such as cutting hedges, mowing lawns, weeding flower beds, clearing beds of dead plants and resetting them. All of this I thoroughly enjoyed, and above all the job was very healthy, through constantly being in the open air.'

The booklet *Working Holidays* has a section on domestic work in Great Britain, which lists a number of hotel and holiday camp organisations that recruit seasonal staff.

Teaching   Temporary positions for assistant teachers and matrons may sometimes be available in preparatory schools. One organisation which may have notice of vacancies is:

Gabbitas, Truman and Thring, 6–8 Sackville Street,

Piccadilly, London W1X 2BR (telephone: 071-734 0161).

Gabbitas, Truman and Thring is a non-profit-making company and the oldest established educational charity in the UK. They offer parents and young people an individual counselling service, for which a fee is charged, on all aspects of education, school and course selection, higher education and careers.

As part of their service Gabbitas, Truman and Thring can advise on the advantages and disadvantages of taking what they call a GAP year. They can advise on sponsorship opportunities and work placements as well as study opportunities at independent colleges.

In addition, school-leavers are recruited for general classroom assistance posts in preparatory schools, and there are also opportunities to work in a non-teaching capacity as assistant matrons or assistant house staff. Those interested in this should ask Gabbitas, Truman and Thring to include their names on the IAPS (Incorporated Association of Preparatory Schools) List, which is circulated to heads looking for school-leavers.

Youth hostels

There are vacancies sometimes for people aged 18 or over to assist wardens in youth hostels, but these are normally filled by the spring. Further information about posts can be obtained by contacting the Youth Hostels Association, Trevelyan House, 8 St Stephen's Hill, St Albans, Hertfordshire AL1 2DY (telephone: 0727 55215).

Youth Training

Youth Training aims to help 16–18 year-olds to prepare for work and to improve their chances of getting and keeping a job. Schemes can last for two years and offer a range of work experience and training in different working environments. An allowance is paid to each trainee on the programme. Youth Training offers a bridge from school to the world of work. Many industries and employers use it as a means of training young people before enrolling them as full-time employees. Details of YT can be obtained from your nearest Careers Office or Jobcentre.

Further information

Directory of Summer Jobs in Britain, published annually by Vacation Work, 9 Park End Street, Oxford OX1 1HJ (telephone: 0865 241978). £7.95. Contains details of voluntary service opportunities, teaching jobs, office work and casual jobs: 30,000 vacancies listed at employers' request.

Opportunities in the 'GAP' year, published by the Independent Schools Careers Organisation (ISCO), 12a–18a Princess Way, Camberley, Surrey GU15 3SP (telephone: 0276 21188). £3 including postage. Sections include office work, voluntary work at home and abroad, pre-university work in engineering and science, attachment to the armed services, etc.

Working Holidays, published annually by the Central Bureau. The book contains an extensive section on Great Britain, with opportunities for paid and unpaid work listed under the headings of Archaeology, Au Pairs/ Nannies, Children's Projects, Community Work, Conservation, Domestic Work, Farm work and Fruit-picking, Leaders and Guides, Teachers, Instructors, Workcamps and General. Practical information is given on cheap travel, accommodation and publications. *Working Holidays* is recognised as the 'bible' of holiday jobs, containing exhaustive information on the jobs themselves – the nature of the work, dates, application deadlines, details of salary or pocket money, whether board, accommodation or insurance is provided – also details of the employers themselves, their aims, philosophies and international representation and all the supportive information. In over 300 pages there is information on paid and short-term voluntary work in Britain and over 100 other countries around the world, including details of entry regulations, any work or residence permits necessary and how to obtain them, travel and accommodation details, addresses of embassies, tourist offices, youth hostels and youth and student travel information centres. £7.95 plus £1.50 postage and packing from the Central Bureau for Educational Visits and Exchanges, Seymour Mews, London W1H 9PE (telephone: 071-486 5101).

8E • ADVENTURE COURSES AND HOLIDAYS

In order to taste the excitements of adventure, you have no need to go abroad. There are many organisations that provide challenging courses and opportunities for physical endeavour and achievement. After the academic grind, such courses have given many young people the chance of discovering a new dimension in themselves.

Adventure is not a male prerogative, as one student makes clear:

'I went on a girls' cruise on the Malcolm Miller *for a fortnight in November. The weather was awful but that added to the fun. It was hard work and you have to put up with a certain amount of hardship, but it is worth it for the pure sense of achievement. Also you build up a sense of companionship and really enjoy trips ashore. On my voyage, we had a bad storm in mid-Channel which was exhilarating rather than frightening; an unforgettable experience.'*

STA Schooners, 2a The Hard, Portsmouth PO1 3PT (telephone: 0705 832055). Offers 13-day adventure training courses for young people aged 16–24 on the sail training schooners *Sir Winston Churchill* and *Malcolm Miller*. Courses start in March.

Further information   *The Traveller's Handbook*, published by WEXAS International Ltd, 45 Brompton Road, Knightsbridge, London SW3 1DE (telephone: 071-589 0500/3315). Lists organisations with youth expedition and adventure interests. It is available to members of the Association, and can be purchased by non-members of WEXAS.

8F • SECRETARIAL AND OTHER COURSES

A year off can be an opportunity to acquire skills that will be useful for securing employment later on, or which will make you more independent and resourceful. Both men and women may find it an advantage to take a secretarial course: nowadays the ability to type is useful for anyone. Most colleges of further education offer secretarial courses, and these range in length from three months (intensive typing) to one academic year. Many of these courses are free to local residents under 19, and grants are often available to those over 19. You should contact your local careers officer to find out about courses in your area and look at the prospectuses that can be obtained in public libraries or from school careers departments.

Details about cookery and housecraft courses can also be obtained from the local college of further education or careers office. Secretarial, cookery, computing and business studies courses, amongst others, are offered by many private colleges of further education throughout the UK. These can be expensive, so it is important to make enquiries about suitability and value.

Skill in teaching English as a foreign language (TEFL) is also useful for those who want to work abroad later, and for those who would like to get summer jobs in Britain teaching young foreign students. Those who have a basic TEFL qualification have an advantage over the totally inexperienced. Four-week courses for those over 20 are provided by, among others, the International Teacher Training Institute, International House, 106 Piccadilly, London W1V 9FL (telephone: 071-491 2598).

Bridging the gap courses
Business studies, information technology, art, languages, and other courses for those who have recently left school and who wish to embark upon a practical course of training, or wish to 'take a year out' before going to university. A wide range of courses is available, including computing, communication studies, languages, art and graphic design, and an introduction to business studies. Some of the courses will lead to public examinations such as the Royal Society of Arts and the London Chamber of Commerce.

Contact Your local colleges of further and higher education.

9 ● A YEAR OFF . . . ABROAD

Europe

Most students like the idea of spending part or all of their year off working and travelling abroad. 'Abroad' can mean Europe; the familiar countries (Spain, France, Germany, Italy), and opportunities have expanded in Russia, Poland and the Baltic states as the political situation in Eastern Europe has eased. But it must be stressed that jobs are very difficult to find in Eastern Europe, and the best way of spending a year or so there may be in voluntary work, youth camps and in teaching English in schools.

Holiday and voluntary work in Europe can be a most enjoyable and rewarding experience. It provides an opportunity to meet people of different social, educational and national backgrounds; to learn new skills; to improve one's understanding of the language and culture of the country; and to earn some cash.

Among the range of jobs available and that can be applied for are these:

Excavation and restoration work. Age is 16 plus.	**Archaeology**
Ages 18–30, mostly for women.	**Au pairs**
Short-term voluntary work in community service can be of great educational and social value, and there are many opportunities to actively participate in improving community life. Projects include helping to run play schemes	**Community work**

for able-bodied or handicapped children, helping with the elderly, working with immigrant communities, and taking children from deprived inner city areas on countryside holidays. Volunteers receive board and lodging and may also be given pocket money and travel expenses. Projects are run at Christmas and Easter as well as June–October. Age 18 plus.

Conservation work
Projects can involve countryside conservation, the restoration of old buildings and environmental repair. Projects tend to last two to six weeks. Accommodation is usually given in village halls, schools or farms. Age range 13 plus.

Couriers
Holiday companies employ couriers to act as representatives and guides. Some knowledge of the language is essential. Age 18 plus.

Farm work
Agricultural jobs of all kinds. Age range 16 plus.

Teachers
For English language teaching in most European countries. Age range 18 plus.

Workcamps
International workcamps provide an opportunity for people of different backgrounds to live and work together and to provide a service to the community. The work is usually for five to six days per week. Some workcamps have shorter working hours and an organised study programme concerned with social problems or wider international issues. Workcamps are organised June–September and at Christmas and Easter. Age 18 plus; some opportunities also exist for ages 15 plus.

Further information
Of the guidebooks which help students to find places in the USA, in Europe and elsewhere in the world, these can be recommended:

Working Holidays and *Volunteer Work*, available from the Central Bureau and the *Directory of Summer Jobs Abroad*, the *Summer Employment Directory of the USA* and other guides published by Vacation Work.

Those who intend to work or travel abroad would do well to arrange insurance cover in the event of accident, sickness or disablement. Some workcamps and voluntary agencies arrange insurance cover for those taking part in their projects, but this is not always the case. Those who are registered as insured persons under the UK National Insurance Scheme are entitled to free medical treatment in EC countries. The certificate of entitlement, form E111, which has to be filled in for this purpose prior to leaving the UK, is available from post offices. ISIS (International Student Insurance Service) provides reasonably priced insurance cover for young people travelling or working abroad. Details of ISIS are obtainable from Endsleigh Insurance Services Ltd, Endsleigh House, Ambrose Street, Cheltenham, Gloucester GL50 3NR.

Insurance

9A • VOLUNTARY SERVICE AND CONSERVATION PROJECTS

Voluntary service   Undertaking voluntary service or work with a charity is one of the most challenging ways of spending a year out, whether at home or abroad. It can offer an opportunity to help others and put something back into the community. The pay may be little or nothing – indeed, some voluntary work projects will cost you money – but great non-monetary benefits are on offer. You are sure to find out more about yourself and develop valuable personal skills – skills that can be used once you return to the world of education.

Motivation   Voluntary work must never be considered as a free or cheap holiday, or an easy way of getting a reference or filling out your UCCA form. It is important to have a heartfelt desire to do the work in question. So much the better if you have a religious or political motivation that has encouraged you to volunteer. If, for example, you wish to volunteer in Eastern Europe you should already have some knowledge of the politics of that region and be committed to the long-term rehabilitation of these countries, rather than offering easy, quick-fix aid.

Eligibility   The agencies that offer voluntary work programmes rarely take just anyone. They can be very demanding and will expect to be convinced of your interest in the subject before they will offer you a place. Sometimes it is necessary to have your application endorsed by your school or, as many programmes are church-run, by your church.

Not all voluntary service opportunities are suitable for school-leavers. Some organisations, such as VSO, take only qualified and experienced people. VSO also usually require a two-year commitment and Project Trust a one-year stay (details later). However, most programmes run for three or four weeks between May and September.

Most voluntary work programmes are unpaid, and some require you to contribute towards travel and accommodation. A very few programmes pay a small wage.

Pay

Details of voluntary service projects can be obtained from the books *Volunteer Work* and *Working Holidays*. For summer projects it is advisable to apply very early, often in January or sooner.

Further details

Some enterprising school-leavers have made their own private arrangements about finding voluntary work abroad, through their school, through friends living abroad or through their church.

Private enterprise

One such student wrote:
'I worked in a South African mission hospital – it had links with my local parish church who suggested that I should write to them.'

In most of these private arrangements students have to pay their own fares, although help may be found from the local Rotary Club or similar organisations.

By far the best guides to volunteer work are published by the Central Bureau.

Using the guides

The guides are:

Volunteer Work, the fifth edition of which now contains full information on volunteer work with over 100 organisations in the UK and 150 countries around the world. It includes a personal checklist which can be used to evaluate your potential, advice on choosing a volunteer programme and gives practical information on preparation and help for returning volunteers. It costs £7.99 and is available direct from the Central Bureau (£9.49 including UK postage, £10.49 including postage to Europe and £12.99 including worldwide airmail postage).

The second book, *Working Holidays*, is also published by the Central Bureau. The latest edition has 310 pages of information and advice on voluntary service, including short-term work, community work and workcamps, plus paid work opportunities in many countries. It costs £7.95 and is available from the Central Bureau (£9.45 including UK postage, £11.45 including postage to Europe and £13.95 including worldwide airmail postage).

Central Bureau for Educational Visits & Exchanges Seymour Mews, London W1H 9PE (telephone: 071-486 5101). Fax 071-935 5741.
3 Bruntsfield Crescent, Edinburgh EH10 4HD (telephone: 031-447 8024). Fax 031-452 8569.
16 Malone Road, Belfast BT9 5BN (telephone: 0232 664418/9). Fax 0232 661275.

Australian Trust for Conservation Volunteers (ATCV)

ATCV is the means by which voluntary manpower can be harnessed to benefit the environment.

The Trust is concerned with environmental problems such as salinity, soil erosion, and loss of native habitat, native flora and fauna.

ATCV aims to:
1 Promote practical conservation projects throughout Australia by involving people on a voluntary basis in the management and care of their environment.

2 Assist local groups with management of conservation projects.
3 Link landholders and volunteers in conservation-orientated projects.
4 Develop training programmes for volunteers to acquire practical skills.
5 Develop links with schools relating conservation projects to curriculum subjects and work experience, eg practical involvement on LandCare projects.

Overseas volunteers are invited to participate by undertaking an ECHIDNA Package.

The ECHIDNA Package provides volunteers with the opportunity to undertake conservation projects with the ATCV. The minimum package is for six weeks with the option to extend if vacancies are available.

Enquiries should be forwarded to the address provided, with two response-international coupons to cover return mail.

ATCV has offices in Melbourne, Ballarat, Bendigo, Adelaide, Sydney and Brisbane. The ATCV was formed in Victoria in 1982, and has developed a well-organised and efficient infrastructure. In the last twelve months ATCV volunteers have worked in Victoria, New South Wales, Tasmania, South Australia, Queensland and the Northern Territory.

Australian Trust for Conservation Volunteers, PO Box 423 Ballarat, Victoria 3350 (telephone: (International Access Code 010 61) 53 33 1483). The fax number is 010 61 53 33 22 90.

Action Health 2000

Contact Gate House, Gwydir Street, Cambridge CB1 2LG (telephone: 0223 460853).
Necessary qualifications Professional health qualifications. Volunteers need to be resourceful and have non-

verbal communication skills.

Type of service Health services.

Countries India, Tanzania, Zambia, Uganda, China.

Length of service 3 months to 2 years.

Accommodation Simple housing, local food; travel costs and pocket money provided.

ATD Fourth World

Contact The General Secretary, 48 Addington Square, London SE5 7LB (telephone: 071-703 3231).

Type of service *Aide à Toute Détresse* is an international movement founded in 1958 in France, and established as a charity in the UK in 1963. Workers and their families who live in extreme poverty increasingly depend on others, and despite their hopes and efforts are denied the means of being fully active members of society. In every country, these families constitute the Fourth World. ADT works alongside the most disadvantaged and excluded families to protect and guarantee the rights of families to family life and education.

Workcamps and working weekends are arranged, where volunteers work on building, decorating, gardening, secretarial and translation work at centres and homes. For volunteers who are able to stay longer, it is sometimes possible to take part in projects at nurseries, skill centres, libraries, youth and children's clubs and on family holidays. The centres are in Africa and Asia.

Necessary qualifications Age 18 plus. There are no minimum requirements, professionally or academically; everyone is welcome, including couples with families.

Length of service At least six months.

Accommodation Volunteers on workcamps/working weekends contribute towards food and accommodation. Permanent members are provided with accommodation, food, pocket money after three months' service, and a minimum wage after one year.

Contact The Overseas Secretary, PO Box 49, Baptist House, 129 Broadway, Didcot, Oxfordshire OX11 8RT (telephone: 0235 512077).

Baptist Missionary Society Programme

Type of service 28:19 The Action Teams offer opportunities for those aged 18–25 years to find out about life in a different country, share in practical work with a local Baptist Church and be involved in their mission to the community around them.

From mid-September teams of six get a month's training, then a full six months living in another part of the world followed by two months back in Britain sharing their experiences with churches and youth groups.

Countries Teams have gone to Jamaica, India, Bangladesh, France, Brazil, Italy and El Salvador.

Cost Participants contribute to travel and training expenses. BMS provides accommodation within Britain and the partner country.

Contact Telephone 0491 39766 to be put on BTCV's mailing list for a brochure which will be ready in April.

British Trust for Conservation Volunteers

Type of service One- and two-week International Conservation Working Holidays. Volunteers join projects in France, Spain, Germany, Norway, Italy, Greece, Iceland the USA and Canada. Project leaders generally speak English, although it's useful to know the local language. Prices are roughly £60 per week, excluding travel to the pick-up point.

BTCV does not offer long-term places abroad.

Contact The Experience Programme Adviser, Partnership House, CMS, 157 Waterloo Road, London SE1 8UU (telephone: 071-928 8681).

Church Missionary Society

CMS can help people in the 18–30 age range through its 'Experience camps' These run during August and take place in parts of Africa, Asia and the Middle East.

'Britain experience placements' are for those in the 18–30 age range and provide opportunities to gain experience of a culturally different part of Britain to what they are used to. Placements are for 6–18 months.

'Overseas experience placements' are aimed at those in the 21–30 age range. Placements are mostly in Asia though a few are available in Africa. Placements are for periods of 6–18 months. A professional qualification or degree is normally required.

CMS provides the costs of training and pays living and pocket money, but participants are responsible for other costs.

Earthwatch Europe	**Contact** Belsyre Court, 57 Woodstock Road, Oxford OX2 6HV (see page 119).

Friends of Israel Education Trust

Contact Director, Friends of Israel, 25 Lyndale Avenue, London NW2 2QB (telephone: 071-435 6803).

Necessary qualifications Over 18; no knowledge of Hebrew is required. Must be in good health.

Type of service The Bridge in Britain scholarship programme is sponsored by the Friends of Israel Educational Trust. The scheme is designed to promote a working knowledge and a sympathetic understanding of the problems and achievements of the State of Israel and its peoples. Up to 12 school-leavers are offered a passage to Israel and free board and lodging for five creative months in Israel. Under the scheme, award winners are afforded:

• a working place on a kibbutz (collective farm)
• two months' community service in a development town
• seminars and organised tours, as well as free time to travel round the country
• experience of an archaeological dig – now an optional extra – at the participant's expense.

The back-up of specialist helpers will be available

throughout the period in Israel. Places are open to all, irrespective of sex, religion or creed.

Conditions All applicants have to explain their reasons for wishing to stay in Israel in a 400- (at least) word essay, to be submitted no later than 1 July, each year.

How to apply A curriculum vitae including date of birth, address, home telephone number, religion, academic achievements, interests and future plans, and a passport-size photo.

Short-listed candidates will be individually interviewed.

International Agricultural Exchange Association

If you want to work abroad and you have a background in farming, IAEA provides opportunities. You can live with a host family in another part of the world and work with them in their agricultural or horticultural enterprises.

It is a challenge that brings benefits educationally and personally. You have the chance to learn about agriculture in other parts of the world, try other ways of life and if interested, learn a different language.

Founded in 1963, the International Agricultural Exchange Association is a democratic, non-profit-making organisation which works closely with rural youth organisations and agricultural colleges in many of its member countries. These countries are Austria, Belgium, Denmark, Finland, France, Germany, Iceland, Ireland, Luxemburg, Netherlands, Latvia, Norway, Sweden, Switzerland, United Kingdom, Japan, Canada, USA, Australia and New Zealand. Participants have come from all these countries, although not all have reciprocal host families.

The programmes available vary in length from six to fourteen months, the longer ones being to two countries; the longest stay in one country is nine months. From the

United Kingdom, volunteers travel to Australia, New Zealand, Canada, United States and Japan.

Categories are available in:

Agriculture Farm jobs are available; applicants must have good practical experience in general farming.

Agri-mix You will work both on the farm and in the household, you must have some general practical experience and an interest in agriculture and home management.

Horticulture You will work in orchards, greenhouses or with vegetables and need to have good practical experience in horticulture.

Horti-mix You will work both with horticulture and in the household. You must have good general practical experience and an interest in home management.

Home management You will work in the house and cook, clean, look after the children and help in the garden. You need to have good experience and an interest in general housekeeping.

Within each of these categories you can also choose the type of farm you would like to work on, eg dairy, sheep, beef or arable, fruit, vegetables or landscape gardening. IAEA aims to find you a host family who will best suit your experience, wishes and interests.

For each programme available, there is a total cost that covers all flights, airport taxes, insurances, stop-overs (these are usually in Bangkok, Singapore or Hawaii), transportation from point of arrival in host country to host family's farm, two-year membership of IAEA, pre-departure information meeting, orientation seminar in host country on arrival and IAEA administration fees.

While you are on the farm you undertake paid work, being expected to do a five-day week, living as part of the family. All the programmes also include unpaid time off for holidays. This varies from three to eight weeks according to the programme you choose.

IAEA UK Service Office, YFC Centre, National Agricultural Centre, Stoneleigh Park, Kenilworth, Warwickshire CV8 2LG (telephone: 0203 696578). Fax 0203 696684.

Involvement Volunteering is to travel and be involved in one or more volunteer activities in countries along the route as an individual, in pairs, in groups or in teams. Operations now extend to Australia, California, the Central Americas, Fiji, Germany, Hawaii, India, New Zealand and Thailand.

Involvement Volunteers Assoc Inc

Costs On payment of the initial or application fee of AU$100 for '93, the potential volunteer receives a suggested programme of volunteer placements within the volunteer's budget as well as the Involvement Volunteering newsletter, which is published four times each year and sent to intending volunteers to illustrate what is available for the coming year. To confirm acceptance of a programme with any number of Individual Volunteer Placements (IVPs) or Special Individual Volunteer Placements (SIVPs) in Australia, Fiji, India, New Zealand and/or Thailand the cost is AU$250. Pairs of volunteers who participate and travel together get a reduction.

For **IVPs** or **SIVPs** in California and Hawaii the cost is US$250. In Germany and the rest of Europe it is DM250.

Team Tasks (TTs) cost AU$75, US$60 or DM80 per week in all countries.

Some IVPs and SIVPs and TTs may have special 'local' costs as shown in the newsletter.

Internal travel in Australia is available to IVI's volunteers at a discount to take volunteers to placements along a route, and so enable the volunteer to combine touring with volunteering. In the event of a family emergency, IVI provides the means for families to contact their relatives volunteering in Australia.

Scuba diving A PADI open-water scuba diving course is available in Australia to IVI volunteers at a discount, providing four days with three nights on board a boat, out on the famous Barrier Reef.

Paid work is sometimes available in Australia to volunteers with working holiday visas in limited areas as the seasonal demands of the fruit industry permit.

For further information, contact Involvement Volunteers Assoc Inc, PO Box 218, Port Melbourne, Victoria 3207, Australia (telephone and fax: 010 613 646 5504).

The Missions to Seamen

Contact The General Secretary, The Missions to Seamen, St Michael Paternoster Royal, College Hill, London EC4R 2RL (telephone: 071-248 5202).

Necessary qualifications Applicants must be at least 18 and hold a valid driving licence. They should be Anglican or a member of another Christian denomination and prepared to participate fully in Anglican ministry and worship.

Type of service Work based on clubs in ports.

Countries Britain, Europe, Far East and Australia, the USA and Africa.

Average length of service One year.

Applications Should be received in March to start in August or September of the same year.

Annual recruitment 30.

Accommodation and pay Free board and accommodation provided, travel fares are paid for by the organisation and volunteers receive about £30 per week. Overseas pay is adjusted to the cost of living.

Youth organisations are into overseas conservation work in a big way, and at least one, **Raleigh International**, offers short-term expeditions for adults. Tall-ship trips are a thing of the past, and Raleigh now concentrates on conservation and community projects. The price, however, is very high indeed; you'll need to be a well-heeled 'year-off-er' to afford this one.

Raleigh International

Contact Raleigh International, Raleigh House, 27 Parson's Green Lane, London SW6 4HS (telephone: 071-376 8536).

Contact The Director, Project Trust, Hebridean Centre, Ballyhough, Isle of Coll, Argyll PA78 6TE (telephone: 08793 444).

Project Trust

Necessary qualifications Applicants should be British, aged between 17 years 3 months and 19 years 6 months at the time of going abroad, and possess a high standard of intellectual and practical ability. They must be in full-time secondary education at the time of application.

Type of service Volunteers work in social service projects, such as orphanages, homes for physically or mentally handicapped, at schools, on farms, with refugees, and at outward-bound schools.

Countries Central America, Africa, Middle and Far East and Australia.

Minimum length of service One year. Volunteers go abroad in August/September and return the following summer.

Applications Should be made in writing and should be received by 1 November. Applicants attend a preliminary discussion held in various parts of the country, which is then followed by a week's selection course on the Isle of Coll.

Annual recruitment of school-leavers 200.

Accommodation and pay Free board and accommodation provided, travel fares outside the UK and insurance paid for by Project Trust. The cost per volunteer for 1993 is £3,250. £2,750 is raised by the volunteer, with help from Project Trust if necessary.

Voluntary Service Overseas

Contact VSO, 317 Putney Bridge Road, London SW15 2PN (telephone: 081-780 2266).

Necessary qualifications A degree or diploma or professional qualification is essential. Additional work or experience is required in most cases. Age 20–70.

Type of service The programme is confined to qualified volunteers who work in the fields of education, agriculture, the health services, technical projects, and social and business development.

Countries Over 50 developing countries in Africa, the Pacific, the Caribbean and Asia.

Minimum length of service Two years.

Applications Applications accepted throughout the year.

Annual recruitment Qualified volunteers: approximately 750. Of these just under 40% will work in education.

Accommodation and pay VSO pays fares and various grants. The overseas employer provides accommodation and a salary based on local rates.

Free literature giving details of skills and qualifications required and the terms of service is available from the Enquiries Unit.

Overseas opportunities

BMMF International (UK) 186 Kennington Park Road, London SE11 4BT. A three-month programme for young committed Christians.

Coral Cay Conservation Programme Sutton Business Centre, Restmor Way, Wallington, Surrey SM6 7AH (telephone: 081-669 0011): qualified divers are needed to help survey a proposed marine park in Belize's coral reef, which is coming under threat from pollution and tourism. One-month projects run throughout the year.

Operation Mobilisation Quinta, Weston Rhyn, Os-

westry, Shropshire SY10 7LT (telephone: 0691 773388): one- to twelve-month missions in most parts of the world.
United Society for the Propagation of the Gospel (USPG) 157 Waterloo Road, London SE1 8XA: a year for Christians to experience the work of the Church overseas in many parts of the world.
The Winant Clayton Volunteers Association See page 168.

Volunteer Work (£7.99, plus £1.50 postage): this book is a detailed guide to voluntary service opportunities ranging from three months to three years. The book has information on 100 organisations requiring volunteers for projects both in the UK and 150 countries overseas. Many of the projects listed require those with skills/ experience, but there are openings for those without.

Further information

The information provided on each voluntary service organisation includes its origin and philosophy, countries in which projects operate and details of past and current projects. It also details the qualities and qualifications required of would-be volunteers, plus the period of service and pay (if any) and conditions involved.

The book also has much background information on subjects such as the fundamentals of volunteering, pre-departure preparation, passports, visas, permits, travel, insurance and social security. There is also help and advice for returning volunteers.

Home from Home (£6.99 plus £1.50 postage): this book is a guide to homestays and exchange trips in all parts of the world. There is detailed information on organisa-tions that can arrange stays with families both as a paying guest or on an exchange arrangement.

The information provided includes the full name and address of each organisation, type of visit arranged and countries catered for. There are also details of age limits, lengths of visit, dates available, language requirements, language tuition and what overseas representation is provided.

Practical exchange information provided includes details on travel, passports, visas, customs, health and insurance, together with tips on what is expected of those who undertake an exchange trip.

Both available from the Central Bureau for Educational Visits and Exchanges, Seymour Mews, London W1H 9PE (telephone: 071-486 5101).

9 B • WORKCAMPS, PEACECAMPS AND SUMMER PROJECTS

Workcamps, peacecamps and projects that are concerned with protecting the environment provide a wonderful opportunity for people who have varied and different social, cultural and economic backgrounds to enjoy themselves working on common projects that benefit local communities.

Volunteer service brings together people from different races and nations; these volunteers not only help people who are less fortunate, but the experience also greatly aids personal growth and awareness of social responsibilities.

Workcamps provide opportunities for volunteers to learn about the history, cultural life and people of other lands. The camps, which run from four to six weeks (April to October and occasionally at Christmas and Easter) are generally for 16 to 19 year-old students. The personal responsibility is serious, for the participants run the camps, organise their work and lead the discussions. There are also youth workcamps for younger groups of 13 to 16; these are generally more centrally organised.

The type of work done by volunteers varies a lot, and depends on the country or area in which the camp is situated. Jobs can involve gardening, road-building, securing water supplies, making adventure playgrounds and taking part in conservation and community projects. Some of the projects that recent volunteers have been on include building schools and clinics, repairing roads, famine-relief, helping at refugee camps. People have helped in countries such as: India, Thailand, Nepal, Sri Lanka, Ghana, Nigeria, Senegal and Bangladesh.

The manual work undertaken on camps means that volunteers must be fit. The work is usually for seven to eight hours per day, five or six days per week. A few camps have shorter working hours and an organised study programme either concerned with social problems or dealing with wider international issues. Accommodation is provided on almost all workcamps, often in schools, community centres, hostels or under canvas. Living conditions vary considerably and can be basic. Food is usually provided, often on a self-catering basis with volunteers preparing and cooking meals. Most international workcamps consist of 10–30 volunteers from several countries. English is often the working language, especially in Europe, although a knowledge of the country's language is sometimes essential, especially for community work; the other principal working language is French. Volunteers generally arrange and pay for their own travel, and may be expected to make a contribution towards the cost of board and lodging.

Working Holidays, published by the Central Bureau, has details of workcamps in over 35 countries. Details of the book are given in the previous section on voluntary service.

International contacts

Each European nation organises international volunteer activity in its own country. Volunteers undertake light to not-so-light construction and renovation work on behalf of the socially, physically and mentally underprivileged. The minimum length of service is two to four weeks, depending on the duration of the camp, though a longer-term commitment is sometimes possible. Salary and travel expenses are not provided, but volunteers are given free board, accommodation and insurance cover.

Applications should be made to one of the national organisations given below:

Austria
SCI, Schottengasse 3a 1/4/59
1010 Vienna IVS
Austria

Belgium
Bouworde
Tiensesteenweg 145
3200 Kessel-10
Leuven
Belgium

Natuur 2000
Flemish Youth Federation for the Study and
  Conservation of Nature
Bervoetstraat 33
2000 Antwerp
Belgium

France
Jeunesse Quart Mond
Alternative 114
29 rue du Stade
Champeaux
77720 Mormant
France

Centre d'Information et de Documentation Jeunesse
101 Quai Branly
Paris 75740
Cedex 15
France

Chantiers de Jeunes, Provence Cote d'Azur
La ferme Giaume – 7 Avenue Pierre de Coubertin
06150 Cannes La Bocca
France

Germany
Studenten Reise Service
Alexanderplatz 25
PSF 57
Berlin 1026
Germany

Artu Berliner Gesellschaft für Studenten und
    Jugendaustausch GmbH
Hardenbergstrasse 9
1 Berlin 12
Germany

Internationale Jugendgemeinschaftsdienste EV
Kaiserstrasse 43
5300 Bonn 1
Germany

Aufbauwerk der Jugend In
    Deutschland EV
Bahnhofstrasse 26
3550 Marburg/Lahn
Germany

Greece
Service Civil International
Erika Kalamatzi
59 Kefallimias Street
11 251 Athens
Greece

Italy
Associazione Italiana Soci
    Costruttori
via Caesare Battisti 3
20071 Casalpusterlengo
Milan
Italy

Comunita Emmaus
Segretariato Campi di Lavoro
Via la Luna 1
52020 Pergine Valdarno
Arezzo
Italy

Netherlands
Exis Centre for Youth Activities
Prof Tulpstraat 2
1018 HA Amsterdam
PO Box 15344
1001 MH Amsterdam
Netherlands

ICVD
Pesthuislaan 25
1054 RH Amsterdam
Netherlands

Norway
Nansen International Centre
Barnegården Breivold
1433 Vinterbro
Norway
(see entry on pages 166–7)

Portugal
Associaccao de Turismo Estudantil & Juvenil
PO Box 586
4009 Porto Cedex
Portugal

Companheiros Construtores
Rua Pedro Monteiro 3–1
Coimbra
Portugal

Spain
Club de Relaciones Culturales
   Internacionales
Calle de Ferraz 82
28002 Madrid
Spain

Switzerland
ATD Quart Monde
1733 Treyvaux Switzerland

Gruppo Voluntari della Svizzera Italiana
CP 12
6517 Arbedo
Switzerland

United States
See entries for BUNAC and GAP Activity Projects.

Camp America

Contact Dept ANRO3, 37a Queen's Gate, London SW7 5HR (telephone: 071-589 3223). Arranges for young people (18–35) to work on American summer camps for ten weeks either as counsellors (looking after children) or as camp power workers (working in the kitchen, laundry, office, etc). There are also places for applicants who wish to look after children in American families for ten weeks. Camp America offers free return flight, board and lodging, pocket money and up to six weeks for independent travel.
Closing date for applications End of April. Must be available by 30 June.
Annual recruitment 6,600.

Christian Movement for Peace

Contact CMP, 186 St Paul's Road, Balsall Heath, Birmingham B12 8LZ (telephone: 021-446 5704). CMP runs two- to four-week summer voluntary projects in Britain, Europe and North America, as well as recruiting volunteers for projects in Spain, Poland, Turkey and

North Africa. There is an enormous variety of work available, from renovation and restoration of historic buildings to social work in the inner cities or working with children. The projects offer the opportunity of service in an area of need and provide work in a community atmosphere both with the other volunteers and the local people.

CMP also arranges medium-term voluntary work for periods of six months in EC countries.

Previous experience and knowledge of a foreign language are not usually required.

Minimum age 17 for British and 18 for foreign projects.

Closing date for applications Please send £1's worth of first/second class stamps to the above address for the summer workcamp brochure which is published in April.

Annual recruitment 400.

Concordia (Youth Service Volunteers) is a non-profit-making charity that celebrates its 50th anniversary in 1993. It works in conjunction with European voluntary youth organisations which organise international work-camps in France, Germany, Latvia, Tunisia and Turkey.

Concordia (Youth Service Volunteers)

These camps last 2–3 weeks and take place from the end of June until mid-September. Some camps are available at Easter, usually those in France and Germany. In addition to the summer workcamp programme, work can also be arranged on farms in Norway (for up to three months) and in the French- and German-speaking cantons of Switzerland (for up to two months during March to November). Pocket money is paid in these cases.

Camp conditions Accommodation and conditions vary considerably from camp to camp, depending on the country and what is available: youth hostels, school halls, farm cottages, mountain huts or tents (climate permitting) are all used to accommodate volunteers at different camps. No atttempt is made to provide single-sex dormitories and, unless there are ample facilities, only one room is set aside for use as sleeping quarters. This is normal practice at this type of camp but can come as a bit of a shock to the unprepared. Volunteers must be prepared to cope with simple, often basic, conditions.

The nature of the work varies from camp to camp; many projects are concerned with nature conservation and environmental protection. Others provide work on the restoration of monuments and castles, construction, community and social work, counselling on children's camps and some English language teaching. As a rule, volunteers work a 5- or $5\frac{1}{2}$-day week, though the actual number of hours worked depends on the climate.

Participating in a workcamp certainly challenges the volunteer's skills, inner resources and initiative, and can also be excellent fun. Many volunteers tell us on their return journey that the workcamp was the best thing they had done in a long time.

Fees A registration fee is charged in all cases, but this varies greatly from country to country. As a guideline, fees in 1992 varied from £45 (France) to £30 (Latvia). The registration fee covers your board and lodging, and in most cases insurance against accidents *whilst at the camp*. In addition, many camps make arrangements for sports and social activities, and excursions out of hours and at weekends. A £10 administration fee is charged to cover costs and a deposit of £20 is required. The deposit is refunded upon return to the UK, provided volunteers do not leave camp early or cancel once acceptance by the foreign organisation has been confirmed. If a place is cancelled less than three weeks before the camp start date, a cancellation fee may be charged.

Travel Volunteers pay their own travel costs, and are

responsible for travel arrangements, visas, passports, etc. We would ask that applicants try to be fairly flexible, as the dates of the camps may be changed at a later date due to circumstances beyond our control.

Conditions of service Applicants must be between 18 (17 for France and Germany) and 30 years old. In some cases the upper age limit is 26. As the work is strenuous, physical fitness is essential. Volunteers are expected to participate in all aspects of camp life (cooking in turns for the whole group, for example). A working knowledge of a foreign language may be required, but the lack of this should not deter applicants. English is used as the language of communication at most camps. For most camps, previous voluntary workcamp experience is not required. Experience may be required for some of the new projects that are planned for 1993.

If you are interested in receiving specific camp information, please send an sae to the Overseas Volunteer Co-ordinator, Concordia (YSV) Ltd, 8 Brunswick Place, Hove, East Sussex BN3 1ET (telephone: 0273 772086).

Cotravaux

Contact 11 rue de Clichy, 75009 Paris, France (telephone: 010 331 48 74 79 20).
An officially sponsored body, co-ordinating the activities of organisers of ten French and international workcamp associations for young volunteers and providing general information about them. The camps in France mainly involve manual work (construction, ditch-digging, land-clearing, etc), archaeological digs and the restoration of ancient monuments.
Minimum age 13.

Kibbutzim in Israel

Another type of working holiday is to go to Israel to work on a kibbutz (agricultural collective settlement). The work is varied, some of it agricultural and some on the domestic side. The minimum length of stay is five weeks and applications can be made all the year round. Everyone receives free food and accommodation, but they must pay their own travel fares. A small amount of pocket money may be paid to those going for long periods.

The agencies listed below arrange schemes for young people, mainly between the ages of 18 and 32, to work on kibbutzim. Applicants should be in a good physical and mental condition, and be able to stand up to the conditions of working six days a week, up to eight hours a day.

Kibbutz Representatives, 1a Accommodation Road, London NW11 (telephone: 081-458 9235).

Project 67, 10 Hutton Gardens, London EC1N 8AH (telephone: 071-831 7626). Archaeological digs in Israel are also organised by this agency.

Nansen International Centre, Norway

Breivold is a long-term relief centre for teenagers with deep social and emotional needs ranging from 13 to 18 years old. It is situated on a renovated farm 25 km from Oslo. Help is needed in all aspects of the centre. Applicants with skills of a practical nature and with the initiative to tackle and follow through ideas with the minimum of supervision are needed. Domestic and farm work is also included in the rota, with all volunteers taking turns with the cooking. Cleaning duties and care of the animals is part of the daily routine at Breivold.

There are many possibilities for sports, hobbies, trips, etc, and leaders are expected to motivate the youths in all areas of life. This is the most important aspect of the work as it prepares the young people for the future.

Volunteers at Breivold must be willing to work very hard as the hours are both long and tiring.

Volunteers should preferably be over 22, qualified drivers and have some experience of working with young people. Volunteers receive full board and lodging and 500 Nkr per week. Applicants are expected to stay a year. There is also a special summer project lasting for six weeks, for which the application deadline is the end of March. It takes between three and six months to process the necessary work permits.

Send an international reply coupon for all correspondence, otherwise you may not receive a reply. Apply to the Director at Nansen International Centre, Barnegården Breivold, Nesset - 1400 Ski, Norway.

Contact National Projects Co-ordinator, Toc H, 1 Forest Close, Wendover, Aylesbury, Buckinghamshire HP22 6BT (telephone: 0296 623911).

Toc H

Toc H has been in Germany since the end of the Second World War and provides a range of services to British service personnel and their families based there. For example, Toc H clubs in five locations provide bookshops, a canteen and accommodation facilities.

Volunteers are accepted for a number of projects throughout the year. Recent projects include helping Santa on his tour of Toc H centres around Germany and helping to prepare the Toc H contribution to the German Flower Festival. A fee is charged which goes towards transport and volunteers require their own spending money.

Further details can be found in the Toc H Projects Programme, published twice yearly on the first Monday of March and September.

Minimum age 18. No maximum.

Eligibility Those who have experience working with children and/or experience of Toc H projects in the UK are given preference.

Closing date for applications None, but early application is advised.

Annual recruitment Small number.

Team on Missions

Contact Mr G Armstrong, General Secretary, Irish Methodist Youth Department, Aldersgate House, University Road, Belfast BT7 1NA (telephone: 0232 327191). The Department of Youth and Children's Work requires four volunteers to work together in its Team on Missions throughout Ireland – involvement with youth groups, church activities, summer programmes.

The team year begins on 1 September for a twelve-month period, with the possible option of a further year. Accommodation, expenses and pocket money are provided.

Winant Clayton Volunteers Association

Contact 38 Newark Street, London E1 2AA (telephone: 071-375 0547). This is a summer programme from mid-June to mid-September, involving about eight weeks' work on the eastern side of the United States in urban situations. There are various programmes offering educational, recreational or therapeutic help, ranging from children's play schemes to work with the aged. Volunteers work alongside local people, and are expected to be able to take considerable responsibility for planning and running their own programmes; they should have some experience of similar work in this country. About four weeks' free time is allowed for travel. Board, lodging and pocket money are provided. Small grants are available towards the fare, but volunteers are asked to make a substantial contribution.

Minimum age 19.

Closing date for applications Mid-January. Enclose a large sae.

Annual recruitment 25.

Working Holidays, published by the Central Bureau. This book is regarded as one of the most useful guides to undertaking working holidays (both paid and unpaid) and covers most parts of the world. Areas covered include work on archaeological digs, farms and fruit-picking, conservation projects, kibbutzim and in community projects. There are details of opportunities to work as an au pair or nanny, courier, instructor, teacher or hotel worker. The book also includes information on budget travel and accommodation, sources of job advertising, work permits and visas, language and health problems.

Workcamps Programme, published by the Co-ordinating Committee for International Voluntary Service (UNESCO), 1 rue Moillis, 75015 Paris, France, and revised every two years. Free, on receipt of four international reply coupons.

The following books are available from Vacation Work, 9 Park End Street, Oxford OX1 1HJ (add £1.50 per book to cover postage and packing):

Directory of Summer Jobs Abroad, £7.95
Directory of Summer Jobs in Britain, £7.95
Kibbutz Volunteer, £5.95
The International Directory of Voluntary Work, £8.95
Live and Work in France, £6.95.
Work Your Way Around the World, £9.95.

Further information

The present unemployment situation is not confined to Britain, and jobs on the open market abroad are not always easy to come by, particularly as many countries impose restrictions on foreign workers. Since Britain joined the EC, British citizens do not need to obtain a work permit to work in Belgium, Holland, Denmark, France, Germany, Greece, Ireland, Italy, Luxemburg, Spain and Portugal, but a British citizen intending to work in one of these countries should have a full passport endorsed on page five by the British Passport Office to the effect that the 'holder has right of abode in the UK'. Those intending to work in an EC member state should obtain the pamphlet *Working in Europe* published by the Department of Employment and available at local Job-centres.

We have concentrated in this section on established organisations which have developed schemes that are especially suitable for young people. However, many students have found interesting jobs abroad through friends or relatives. Most of those who found ordinary jobs abroad without using an agency or friends worked in Germany, where it has proved easier to find employment than in, say, France or Sweden. Some students have found interesting work abroad by applying direct to travel firms or tour operators for work as couriers or tour leaders, although it should be stressed that this type of work calls for energy, leadership qualities and fluency in languages.

Leaflets giving advice on employment prospects and listing agencies offering work are issued by many of the national tourist offices in this country.

Applications for jobs abroad should be typed, and be accompanied by an international reply coupon. It is advisable to have a passport-type photograph ready to send, if requested.

16 Bowling Green Lane, London EC1R 0BD (telephone: 071-251 3472). Organises a number of work exchange programmes between the USA, Canada and the UK for students and young people. 1992–93 membership to BUNAC costs £3.50.

British Universities North America Club (BUNAC)

BUNACAMP requires students and non-students between the ages of 19½ (by July) and 35 to work as camp counsellors on American children's summer camps from June to mid/end August. A registration fee of £55 is required. BUNACAMP finds placements for suitable applicants, arranges return flights, visa and insurance. Camps provide board and lodging and a salary of $390 to $450. Applicants must be energetic and hard-working, and have some previous experience of working with groups of children.

BUNACAMP

Work America Programme and **Kitchen and Maintenance Programme** offer students studying at HND level and above in tertiary education the chance to work in a variety of jobs during the summer months (June–September). WAP entitles you to take any job anywhere in the USA and KAMP entitles you to do a variety of non-counselling jobs on summer camps.

WAP/KAMP

This scheme provides a general work permit valid for a six-month period which authorises the student to take up any job anywhere in Canada. To be eligible for this programme applicants must be current students in full-time higher education in this country. Students in their gap year and who are at least 18 can apply if they have

Work Canada

an unconditional place at college for the following autumn.

Work Australia

Work Australia offers young people aged 18–25 (inclusive) the chance to live and work in Australia for up to one year. The programme features a round-trip flight, working holiday visa, Hawaii stop-over (if flying from Los Angeles), ongoing support and assistance, mail forwarding, orientations and two nights' hotel accommodation in Sydney. Applicants must be citizens of the UK, Canada, Holland or Ireland.

For further details of any of the above programmes send your name and address on a postcard to Dept AZ1, BUNAC at the address above.

The Central Bureau for Educational Visits and Exchanges

The Central Bureau is the national office responsible for the provision of information and advice on all forms of educational visits and exchanges; the development and administration of a wide range of curriculum-related pre-service and in-service exchange programmes; the linking of educational establishments and local education authorities with counterparts abroad; and the organisation of meetings and conferences related to professional international experience. The Central Bureau for Educational Visits and Exchanges, Seymour Mews, London W1H 9PE (telephone: 071-486 5101).

Information and advice

The Central Bureau's information and advisory services extend throughout the educational field. In addition, over 20,000 individual enquiries are received and answered each year. Publications cater for the needs of people of all ages seeking information on the various opportunities available for educational contacts and travel abroad.

16–19 Study Bursaries

Those aged between 16 and 19 in full- or part-time education in England and Wales can take advantage of a Project Europe 16–19 Bursary so that they can make a study visit to another European country, related to the work they are doing in their school curriculum. To be eligible, participants must devise their own study project and make their own arrangements for the visit. Application forms are available from the Central Bureau Schools Unit.

IAESTE work placements

The International Association for the Exchange of Students for Technical Experience is an independent worldwide organisation for which the Central Bureau is the UK secretariat. Course-related paid work placements are arranged on an exchange basis for degree level students in fields such as engineering, sciences, agriculture and the applied arts. Placements are available in 59 countries worldwide. Most are for 12 weeks during the summer, although longer-term placements may sometimes be arranged. UK higher education students should apply through IAESTE-UK representatives, provided their university is affiliated to the programme.

PETRA II – initial vocational training

This EC programme provides financial support for 16–27 year olds to benefit from vocational training/work experience in another EC Member State. Short-term placements (3 weeks to 3 months) are aimed at young people who are in initial vocational training leading to recognised qualifications such as BTEC, CGLI, SCOTVEC etc. Longer term work experience placements (3–12 months) are aimed at young people in employment, work seekers or those taking part in an advanced training programme after starting work. (Please note that university students are not eligible.) Individuals who would like assistance in identifying work placements are advised to register their interest with the PETRA National Coordination Unit at the Central Bureau who will forward details of organisations arranging work placements. They may also like to look out for opportunities advertised by project organisers in local or national newspapers.

**English
language
summer camps**

Sixth-formers are required at English language summer camps held in Hungary, Poland and Turkey. The main objective is to provide young people in those countries with the opportunity of practising English learnt in school, and by spending three weeks in the company of British teachers and young people to acquire a deeper awareness of the British way of life. Duties include assisting with the teaching of English as a foreign language, running conversation classes and organising sporting, musical and social activities, including drama, embroidery, folk dancing and singing workshops. Applicants should be native English speakers, aged 16–19, with a sense of responsibility, organisational skill, adaptability to new surroundings, a social nature and an ability and interest in sports and/or drama and music, plus experience in working with children. Camps last for three weeks during July and August. Board and accommodation, sharing with the pupils, is provided. Excursions and visits to places of interest are arranged. Group travel, approximately £220, including insurance and visa, is paid by applicants. Apply to Central Bureau Schools Unit by mid-April.

**Language
Assistants**

English language assistants are assigned to schools or colleges abroad, where their role is to help the teachers of English in every way they can. Although the nature and range of activities involved will vary from post to post, the main tasks of an assistant is to improve pupils' English language skills, particularly listening and speaking, and to present aspects of the anglophone culture they represent. Work is usually carried out in small groups and almost always in close co-operation with the teacher. Applicants must be native speakers of English, aged 20–30. Most applicants will have completed at least two years of a degree or diploma course, usually in the language of the country for which they are applying. The minimum relevant language qualification is an A-level pass or equivalent. For some countries graduates with teaching experience are preferred. Where the number of applicants exceeds the number of posts available preference is given to undergraduates for whom a year abroad is a course requirement.

For those aged 18–20, taking A-levels in French, German or Spanish and thinking of taking a year out between school and higher education, there are posts available as junior language assistants at schools in France, Germany and Spain. They are expected to help with English teaching in schools for up to 12 hours a week, for which they will receive a modest allowance, plus free board and lodging. The number of posts is limited and competition is very strong. Only a very small number of posts are available in Germany. All assistant posts are administered by the Central Bureau's Language Assistant Department.

Junior Language Assistants

This programme offers native speakers of English, French or German an opportunity to get acquainted with the Finnish way of life, living as a member of a family. An essential part of the programme is for participants to teach their mother tongue to the family. Participants are treated as family members and not as employees. Host families include both farming and urban or suburban families who may move into the country for the summer. As well as language tuition, participants are also expected to help with household chores and/or childcare. On farms the work also involves helping with haymaking, milking, gardening and fruit-picking. Board and lodging is provided, plus pocket money for approximately 25 hours' work over a five-day week. One to three months in the

The Finnish Family Programme

summer, or six to twelve months all year. Participants pay their own travel. Applicants should be aged 18–23. Apply to the Central Bureau Vocational and Technical Education Department, Seymour Mews, London W1H 9PE.

Gap Activity Projects (GAP) Limited

GAP organises work opportunities overseas for school-leavers (18–19 age group) during their 'gap' year between leaving school and going on to further education. The aim is to broaden horizons by providing attachments for 6–12 months in another country. Projects for school-leavers include helping the sick, handicapped and de-prived, English language teaching, assisting in schools, conservation and farming, and office work in Australia, Bulgaria, Canada, Chile, China, Czech and Slovak Republics, Ecuador, Falklands, France, Germany, Hong Kong, Hungary, India, Indonesia, Israel, Japan, Malaysia, Mexico, Namibia, Nepal, New Zealand, Pakis-tan, Poland, Romania, Russia, South Africa, Sri Lanka and the USA.

Applicants pay a £15 registration fee, and on selection a GAP fee, which is currently £350. A one- or two–week TEFL course (approx £100–£150) is also required for English teaching. Volunteers receive free board and lodging and in most cases some pocket money at the placement, but are responsible for their own return air fare, insurance and medical costs.

For further information write to Gap Activity Projects, GAP House, 44 Queen's Road, Reading, Berkshire RG1 4BB (telephone: 0734 594914).

France

The French Government Tourist Office, 178 Piccadilly, London W1V 0AL (telephone: 071-499 6911). Publishes a free leaflet entitled *Working in France* which contains useful information and addresses. Write for information.

Le Centre d'Information et de Documentation Jeunesse (CIDJ), 101 Quai Branly, F-75740 Paris, Cedex 15, publishes a leaflet *Chercher un emploi temporaire durant les périodes*.

Zentralstelle für Arbeitsvermittlung, Abteilung Ausland, Feuerbachstrasse 42–46, 6000 Frankfurt am Main 1, Germany, can find two- to three-month summer posts for students aged 18–30. Applicants should have A-level German and be able to provide proof of university enrolment; otherwise they will be liable to tax and national insurance contributions. The GAP Live and Work in Germany Scheme is organised with help from ZAV.

Germany

Camp America recruits young people to work in American summer camps for ten weeks, looking after and/or teaching American children. In return they receive a free transatlantic return flight, board and lodging, and pocket money. Anyone aged between 18 and 35 who wants more details should send a postcard, with their name and address, to Dept ANRO3C, 37a Queen's Gate, London SW7 5HR (telephone: 071-589 3223).

USA and Canada

Directory of Summer Jobs Abroad, published by Vacation Work, 9 Park End Street, Oxford OX1 1HJ (telephone: 0865 241978). Revised annually, £7.95 (plus £1.50 postage). Gives information not only about vacation work, but about workcamps, au pair and paying guest opportunities, and cut-price travel.

Further Information

The Directory of Jobs and Careers Abroad, Vacation Work, £9.95 plus postage (address as above). The definitive guide to permanent careers abroad for people of all ages, from school-leaver to the fully qualified professional.

9D • WORKING IN FRANCE

A number of guides are available for those wishing to find work in France. One of the main ones is *Working Holidays* published by the Central Bureau for Educational Visits and Exchanges. This book gives addresses for organisations that can offer jobs, information on advertising in French newspapers, and details of cheap accommodation in the Paris region.

Working Holidays is available from most larger bookshops or direct from the Central Bureau for Educational Visits and Exchanges, Seymour Mews, London W1H 9PE (telephone: 071-486 5101) for £7.95 plus 1.50 p&p.

Vacation Work Publications have two books that will be of use. *Live & Work in France* is a general guide to finding work in France. *Emplois d'Eté en France* is an annual directory (in French) of holiday jobs.
Some of the many opportunities in France include:

Animateurs

Young people are needed to work as monitors on summer camps for French children. Good conversational French is required, but the positions provide free board and pay pocket money. The work involves general supervision and sports instruction; qualifications in this are desirable. Applications can be made to Association Montaigne, 83 Boulevard de Montmorency, 75016 Paris.

Archaeology

France is home to many archaeological sites. Some of these welcome beginners although for others it is desirable to be studying archaeology or related subjects. Details of digs requiring volunteers are available from the Ministry of Culture, 4 rue d'Aboukir, 75002 Paris.

France has may opportunities for young people (mostly women) to work as au pairs and nannies, chiefly in the main towns and cities. Jobs can be found by answering newspaper advertisements or via agencies. Apart from the UK agencies some French agencies to try are Accueil Familial des Jeunes Etrangers, 23 rue Cherche-Midi, 75006 Paris and Inter-Séjours, 179 rue de Courcelles, 75017 Paris.

Au pairs/ nannying

Those who speak reasonably good French may be able to get a job in a French shop, office or factory. In particular, there are many temporary jobs in Paris in July and August when the local residents take their summer holidays. Jobs can be found through local employment offices (ANPE) or one of the 550 Manpower employment offices to be found in almost every French town and city. The Paris office is at 9 rue Jacques Bingen, 75017 Paris.

Commerce

France has similar opportunities for working on community projects as are found in the UK. These might involve working with the young, the old, the disabled, ethnic minorities or disadvantaged communities.

Community projects

Fruit-picking is a popular form of casual work in France starting with soft fruit in early summer and the enormous grape harvest (known as the vendange) in late September and October. Work can be found in all areas but it is often a matter of asking around on farms etc once in France. Local state employment agencies (the ANPE) know of some vacancies.

Fruit-picking

There are often openings in the French tourist resorts, especially in shops, hotels, restaurants and bars. Many of these jobs are detailed in *Emplois d'Eté en France*. Most opportunities are in the south of France (especially

Tourism

Provence) in summer and in the French Alpine resorts in winter.

| Workcamps and conservation | A wide variety of workcamps are on offer in France. Projects might include renovating an old building for use as a community centre or repairing mountain footpaths. The co-ordinating organisation for many projects is Cotravaux, 11 rue de Clichy, 75009 Paris, France. |

| Couriers | A number of travel companies, such as PGL Adventure, employ young people as couriers to escort under-18s to Europe for a variety of holidays, which range from educational tours to activity and adventure-type holidays. On the latter you will be expected to participate in many of the activities offered, such as canoeing, windsurfing and sailing. |

PGL Adventure employ site couriers to liaise with families at their Freedom of France self-catering campsites. Site couriers also ensure the cleanliness and upkeep of the facilities. Children's couriers run a daily 'Kids Club' to keep the children occupied.
Contact Personnel Department, Freedom of France, 839 Alton Court, Penyard Lane, Ross-on-Wye HR9 5NR (telephone: 0989 767833).

Other organisations employ graduates and undergraduates as resident campsite couriers, children's couriers and nannies on campsites throughout Europe.
Contact Operations Manager, **Canvas Holidays**, 12 Abbey Park Place, Dunfermline, Scotland (telephone: 0383 621000).
Eurocamp Travel Ltd, Canute Court, Toft Road, Knutsford, Cheshire WA16 0NL (telephone: 0565 633844).

| Visas/permits | If you decide to work in France, you are advised to obtain the Department of Employment leaflet *Working* |

in Europe – how to get a job in another EC member state, and what you should know before you accept it. EC nationals may stay in France for up to three months to find a job, and if you do find one, a residence permit must be applied for. Application forms are available from the Préfecture de Police in Paris and from local police stations elsewhere.

The organisations below publish information sheets for young people and students wishing to live or work in France:

Useful addresses

Accueil des Jeunes en France, 12 rue des Barres, F-75004 Paris (for correspondence) or 16 rue du Pont Louis-Philippe/119 rue Saint-Martin, F-75004 Paris (for personal callers)

Centre d'Information et de Documentation Jeunesse (CIDJ), 101 Quai Branly, F-75740 Paris, Cedex 15, France.

An essential handbook is *Live and Work in France* by Mark Hempshell. This costs £6.95 (plus £1.50 postage) and is published by Vacation Work, 9 Park End Street, Oxford OX1 1HJ.

Also by Vacation Work is *Emplois d'Eté en France*, an annual book that gives details about all types of vacation work in France. This costs £7.95 (plus £1.50 postage).

Becoming an au pair provides the opportunity for young people to learn a language and experience a foreign country within the security of a family environment. While most au pair positions are aimed at girls, there are no restrictions on young men applying and getting positions.

While some 20 countries are part of the international au pair scheme, the easiest countries in which to find positions are those within the European Community, where work permits are no longer required.

Au pair posts are generally for three months or more although a limited number are available for shorter periods in the summer.

The work involved varies from light housework and basic cookery to childcare and will take up to five or six hours a day. In return, the family will provide a room, food and some pocket money. You will usually have plenty of free time to attend language classes and take part in social activities.

The qualifications required are minimal. There is a minimum age of 18 (Belgium, Italy, Spain and the UK will accept those near their 18th birthday). A basic knowledge of the language of the host country is useful and essential for France and Germany. Some experience of childcare (such as babysitting, Guide leader, etc) is helpful as is some basic housework and simple cookery.

Advertisements for au pairs appear in many magazines and papers but probably the most widely used is *The Lady*. The most common method of obtaining a post is through one of a number of agencies handling au pair vacancies. There are a number of positive advantages in dealing with an established and reputable agency:

1 They can offer advice and assistance in finding a suitable post. The best will try to match the applicant individually with a suitable family and take a personal interest in ensuring proper arrangements are made regarding terms and conditions of employment, travel and insurance.

2 They have established relationships with corresponding agents in host countries who will be able to introduce local families needing au pairs, providing a point of local contact in an emergency and assist with arrangements for taking up the post.

3 They are experienced in placing young people and therefore are well aware of the problems associated with leaving home and travelling alone, perhaps for the first time.

Applications must be made in plenty of time. Far better to apply early and allow the agency time to find a place than to apply at the last minute when there is less chance of getting a post in the area or even the country of choice. This is especially true in the case of short-term summer positions.

Similarly, the longer you are prepared to stay the better your chances of finding a place in the area and country of your choice.

Finally it is worth pointing out that being an au pair means becoming part of a family. This gives a degree of security which can be an important consideration for both the au pair and her parents. It also brings a degree of responsibility to comply with the standards of the host family, which may be different to those experienced at home. This does not mean lowering personal standards but does imply compromise and a desire to 'fit in'.

L'Accueil Familial des Jeunes Etrangers

23 rue du Cherche-Midi, 75006 Paris, France.

Au pair stays with French families for girls between 18 and 30 years. Summer placements are arranged from one to three months all over France. Applicants must be able to speak some French. Long stays start 1–15 September and 1–15 January. Long duration stays from September to June can also be arranged. The agency also provides accommodation through its paying guest service. Applications to the above address should be made two weeks before the starting date of work.

Aaron Employment Agency

The Courtyard, Stanley Road, Tunbridge Wells, Kent TN1 2RJ (telephone: 0892 546601).

Places au pairs and nannies in Europe and Canada for a minimum of six weeks at any time of the year. Au pairs earn approximately £140 per month for a 30-hour week, five days a week. Nannies earn approximately £320 per month for a 37–42-hour week over five days and must have relevant qualifications or live-in experience. Board and accommodation are provided free of charge.

Anglia Au Pair Agency

70 Southsea Avenue, Leigh-on-Sea, Essex SS9 2BJ (telephone: 0702 471648).

Au pairs are placed in summer posts throughout Europe. Longer stays, ie six months, are easier to arrange. Homestays and paying guest stays are also arranged in Europe, Australia and North America. Applicants should enclose an sae.

Au Pair Care

44 Cromwell Road, Hove Sussex BN3 3ER (telephone: 0273 220261).

This agency places au pairs in America with the full support of the American authorities. A 12-month scheme is open to people aged 18–25 with a driver's licence and some childcare experience. Visa, return flights, medical insurance, $100 per week pocket money, full board and lodging, a two-week paid vacation and the full support of a local counsellor during your stay are all provided. For further information and an application form contact the agency.

Au Pairs – Italy

46 The Rise, Sevenoaks, Kent TN13 1RJ (telephone: 0732 451522).
Places au pairs, mothers' helps, nannies and governesses in Italy. During the summer holidays, girls are required for about three months, occasionally even for one to two months. Normal length of stay throughout the year is six to twelve months, with a few shorter vacancies usually available.
Minimum age 18 years. Send sae for details.

Avalon Agency

5 St Richards Road, Westergate nr Chichester, West Sussex PO20 6RD (telephone: 0243 542383).
Au pair placements are arranged for two months, summer only. Applicants must be 18 or over and be able to speak the language to GCSE standard.

Avalon Agency

53 Station Road, Shalford, Guildford, Surrey GU4 8HA (telephone: 0483 63640).
Au pair placements, £30–40 per week, for 30 hours a week; placements in Europe and the USA. Board and accommodation for childcare and housework.

Canary Islands Bureau

Santiago B1, 4–5 Santa Cruz de Tenerife, Canary Islands. Au pairs (girls only) in Spain for 4–12 months. Duties are housework, childcare, occasionally with language tuition. Three hours daily, with days and evenings off. Applications must be accompanied by photograph, references and international reply coupon.

Contacts

55 rue Nationale, 37000 Tours, France (telephone: 47 20 20 57).

Au pair placements with French families during summer vacation and for up to 12 months.

Minimum age 18. International reply coupon must accompany application.

EIL Au Pair Au Pair/Homestay USA, 'Otesaga', West Malvern Road, Malvern, Worcestershire WR14 4EN (telephone: 0684 562577).

Au pairs arranged in USA and Canada for 18–25s, non-smokers, with driving licence and experience in childcare, for 12-month stays. Pocket money, free return flight and insurance. For further information contact Margaret Pawson, Principal Administration Officer at the address above.

Childcare International Trafalgar House, Grenville Place, London NW7 3SA (telephone: 081-959 3611/906 3116).

Childcare Europe Au pairs, nannies and mothers' helps are placed in France, Italy, Austria, Holland, Spain, Belgium and Switzerland. A commitment of 6–12 months is preferred but there are also opportunities for three-month seasonal placements. Ski au pair positions are available during the winter months. Experience with children is useful. Preferred age range is 18–27 years. Pocket money depends on experience. Full back-up available in country of placement.

Childcare America Visa-supported one year stay in the USA for applicants aged 18–25 years. Childcare experience advantageous; drivers and non-smokers preferred. Choice of host family. Opportunity to attend part-time college course. Local counsellor support. Return air fare and medical insurance paid plus two weeks' vacation. Start any time. Earn $100 per week.

Childcare Canada Live-in family placements in Canada for those with nanny/teaching/nursing qualification.

Minimum one year stay. Age 18+. Support and assistance given throughout stay.

---

37 Queen's Gate, London SW7 5HR (tel: 071-581 2730). Places au pairs in America for a period of 12 months. Pocket money of $100 per week is guaranteed with two weeks off with pocket money during placement. Au Pair America provides return travel to the host family and arranges a visa and medical insurance: applicants must place a deposit which is refunded after completion of placement. Applicants must be aged 18–25, have experience of childcare and hold a full driving licence. For further details contact the above address.

Au Pair in America

Austria
ÖKISTA
Garnisongasse 7
1090 Vienna

European contacts

Belgium
Au Pair/Homestay USA
33 Boslaan
1900 Overijse
Telephone: + 322 687 2450

Denmark
Dansk Experiment
Ryvangs Alle 72
2900 Hellerup
Telephone: + 45 31 62 29 00

France
Experiment-France
89 rue de Turbigo
75003 Paris
Telephone: + 331 42 78 50 03/42 78 48 35
Fax: +331 42 78 01 40

+ indicates international dialling code 010

Germany
Experiment e.V.
Ubierstrasse 30
D-5300 Bonn 2
Telephone: + 49 228 35 82 42

Great Britain
Au Pair/Homestay USA
'Otesaga'
EIL Ltd
West Malvern Road
Malvern
Worcestershire WR14 4EN
Telephone: 0684 562577

Ireland
Experiment in International Living
Courthouse Chambers
27/29 Washington St
Cork
Telephone: + 353 21 275101

Italy
Experiment in International
Living – Italia
Via del Cavallino 8
14100 Asti
Telephone: + 39 141 52 250

Netherlands
Au Pair/Homestay USA
EXIS
Prof. Tulpstraat 2
1018 HA Amsterdam
Telephone: + 31 20 262664

+ indicates international dialling code 010

Norway
Youth Exchange
Rolf Hofmosgate 18
0655 Oslo
Telephone: + 472 67 00 43

Spain
Asociacion Espanola del Experimento
    de Convivencia
Fernandez de los Rios No. 80, 1 DCH
28015 Madrid
Telephone: + 341 549 33 68/544 78 37

Switzerland
The Experiment in International Living
Seestrasse 167
CH 8800 Thalwil
Telephone: + 411 720 54 97

Turkey
Experiment in International Living
ETILER, Nisbetiye Cad. No.15 K.2
80630 Istanbul
Telephone: + 901 163 51 80/157 09 05

+ indicates international dialling code 010

Euroyouth

301 Westborough Road, Westcliff, Southend-on-Sea, Essex SS0 9PT (telephone: 0702 341434).
Paying guest holidays are arranged, with and without language tuition courses. Venues include Austria, Belgium, France, Germany, Italy, Spain, Greece, Turkey and Portugal for groups and individuals. The agency also arranges holiday guest accommodation in Austria, France, Belgium, Germany, Greece, Italy, Spain and Turkey, mostly during the summer holiday period. Accommodation and food are provided in exchange for English conversation. Especially suitable for students

between 16 and 20 years old who want to improve their knowledge of a foreign language. There are few places available on this scheme, and those interested are advised to go as a paying guest if at all possible. Send an sae to the above address for details.

Galentinas

European Au Pair, Mothers' Helps and Nannies (Domestics) Agency. PO Box 51181, GR 145.10 Kifissia, Greece (telephone and fax: 010 301 808 1005).

Minimum length of service One year (summer season 2–3 months). Galentinas provide professional guidance to qualifying candidates seeking one-year positions with carefully screened families in Greece, Europe and the USA. Excellent conditions and benefits, return airfare, medical insurance, etc. No candidate placement fee.

Helping Hands Agency

10 Hertford Road, Newbury Park, Ilford, Essex IG2 7HQ (telephone: 0702 602067).

Places au pairs/mothers' helps throughout Europe and in Canada (as well as in the UK). Applicants should have at least basic childcare experience. Knowledge of the relevant language is highly desired for overseas placements.

Length of service Work is for three months during the summer or minimum six months at other times of the year.

Age 17 to 27.

Pocket money/wages commences at £30–35 per week for au pairs. Full board. Au pairs work five hours a day, six days a week and do some babysitting. This increases considerably for mothers' helps.

Please send an sae for brochure and application form.

Home from Home

Walnut Orchard, Chearsley, Aylesbury, Buckinghamshire HP18 0DA (telephone: 0844 208561).

Female au pairs placed in France, Spain, Italy, Germany,

Switzerland, The Netherlands, Belgium and the UK. Six
months' minimum stay except in the summer.
Minimum age 18 years.

Via S. Stefano, 40125 Bologna, Italy (telephone: 010 39
51 267575).
International Au Pair

Au pairs are placed in the summer (June–September) or
longer term (6–12 months from September) in Italy. The
work is mostly childminding, with some housework.
Pocket money of approximately £30 per week plus full
board and lodging. Around six working hours per day,
with one complete day and two to three evenings free
per week. Applicants should be aged over 18; experience
of babysitting an advantage.

St Patrick's International Youth Centre, 24 Great Chapel
Street, London W1V 3AF (telephone: 071-734 2156).
The agency organises au pair posts in France for English
girls over the summer.
International Catholic Society for Girls

Minimum age 18 years.
Minimum stay Three months. Applications must include
an sae.

---

179 rue de Courcelles, 75017 Paris, France (telephone:
010 331 47 63 06 81).
Inter-Séjours

Au pairs are placed in Austria, Canary Islands, France,
Germany, Italy and Spain. Duties include five hours a
day, six days a week, housekeeping and looking after
children; and two to three evenings a week babysitting.
Work is for three months during the summer, or six
months throughout the year. Applicants should be aged
between 18 and 25 years and have some knowledge of
the language of the country they wish to visit. Pocket
money is around £150 per month in France and Germany.
Paying guests stay with families in France, Spain and
Germany, Italy and the USA. Two to three hours of

lessons per day plus sporting activities and excursions or just family stays with no lessons.

Jolaine Au Pair Agency
18 Escot Way, Barnet, Hertfordshire EN5 3AN (telephone: 081-449 1334).

Au pair and mothers' help placements with families in Europe for 6–12 month stays. Paying guest stays are also arranged in France, Belgium and Spain for a minimum period of one week.

Mothers' help positions are also arranged in Canada for applicants of 18 years or more who have some experience of looking after children.

Mondial Agency
32 Links Road, West Wickham, Kent BR4 0QW (telephone: 081-777 0510/6271).

Au pair posts, girls only, in Austria, France and Spain. Minimum period is six months.

To be a successful au pair, you must be flexible and willing to adapt to a different way of life which may seem rather strange for the first few weeks.

To apply for an au pair position, you should complete the registration form and return it with two photographs, two written references, a CV in the form of a personal letter and a medical certificate to show a good state of health. Mondial then tries to find a suitable family, who will contact applicants direct. This may take several weeks, since families and applicants need to be matched so that both are happy.

Should you wish to withdraw your application at any time, you should inform Mondial immediately.

An engagement fee of £40 is payable when you accept the offer of a suitable position. You will then be able to use the services of agents in Paris, Nice, Vienna or Barcelona if you have any problems.

Austrian Committee for International Educational Exchange, Garnisongasse 7, 1090 Vienna, Austria.

ÖKISTA

Au pair positions with Austrian families in Vienna, main cities and country areas. Au pairs are expected to help with children and do light housework, five/six hours daily plus babysitting two/three evenings per week by arrangement. One day off per week and time to attend German language classes. Board and lodging provided, pocket money of £150 per month.

Stays are for 6–12 months throughout the year but language classes are not available during the summer as courses start in September, January and at Easter time. Two- to three-month stays, without language classes, during the summer. The agency offers au pair programmes including travel in Austria, sightseeing and meetings with other au pairs. Reduced air fares, train tickets and medical insurance available.

ÖKISTA also provides home-stays with Austrian families as paying guests.

Minimum stay Two weeks.

Minimum age 18.

Applicants pay their own fares and insurance.

Registration fee £25.

Applications to the above address.

51, Rue de Carouge 1205 Geneva, Switzerland.

Pro Filia

Places au pairs with families in the regions of France bordering Switzerland and Geneva for stays of 12 months or more.

---

32 Rempart de l'Est, 16022 Angoulême, France (telephone: 010 33 45 95 83 56).

Séjours Internationaux Linguistiques et Culturels

Au pairs placed with families in France, Germany, Italy, Majorca and Spain for a minimum of eight weeks in the summer or for six months from September. Family-study stays can be arranged in the USA for a maximum of three months for girls aged over 18.

Enquiries to SILC, c/o Fay Forrest Evans, 50 Cypress Avenue, Whitton, Middlesex TW2 7JZ (telephone: 081-894 1151). Fax: 081-755 2347. Other enquiries to the French address above.

South-Eastern Au Pair Bureau

Contact 39 Rutland Avenue, Thorpe Bay, Essex SS1 2XJ (telephone: 0702 601911). This is the sister agency to Helping Hands. See page 190 for details.

Students Abroad Ltd

This organisation, established in 1976, specialises in placing young people as au pairs.

Working with their comprehensive network of agents, they match applicants with host families throughout the European Community, South Africa and the USA.

Au pairs live as part of a family, helping with childcare and light housework. Full room and board is provided. Some childcare/babysitting experience is preferred. Basic language skills are preferred but not essential.

As it is not always easy to adjust to living with a family in a different culture, applicants are advised to make sure this is what they want before making a commitment.

Posts in Europe are for a minimum of six months although some two-month summer placements are possible in France, Italy and Spain. Demand for summer posts is high so early application is essential. £30–35 is paid weekly for approximately 30 hours' work. Free time is given for language classes (not available during summer). Minimum age 18, maximum age 30.

To join the USA programme, you must be aged between 18 and 25, have some childcare/babysitting experience, have a full driving licence and be a non-smoker. Posts are available throughout the USA for one year. Flights and medical insurance are paid and applicants have the opportunity to attend a college course. Benefits include two weeks' vacation, a 24-hour local counsellor and $100 per week pocket money for up to 45 hours' work. A refundable good faith deposit is required.

All applicants are required to complete a registration form, which should be returned with eight photographs, two references, a clear medical certificate from their doctor and an introduction letter to the prospective host family.

A £40 service fee is sought from applicants (except applicants for the USA). This is refunded in full in the unlikely event that the applicant does not accept a post. An information pack is also available at the cost of £5. This includes an introduction to the host country, helpful hints on discount travel, work permit/visa requirements, comprehensive health/travel insurance (including free telephone or postal insurance brokerage service), E-111 and a health information booklet.

For information and a registration form, please send a large sae to: Students Abroad Ltd, 11 Milton View, Hitchin, Hertfordshire SG4 0QD (telephone: 0462 438909).

Universal Care

Chester House, 9 Windsor End, Beaconsfield, Buckinghamshire HP9 2JJ (telephone: 0494 678811). Fax 0494 671259.

Universal care specialises in providing opportunities for young people to become au pairs in western European countries. They have associated agents in France, Italy, Spain and Germany who select suitable families for prospective au pairs. Provided that the young person wishes to be placed for at least six months, there is no difficulty in finding a suitable family. Prospective au pairs should write to Universal Care, and will be sent full details of the service together with an application form. They are then required to complete the application form, and return it together with four passport size photographs of themselves, a medical clearance from their doctor, two references and a letter to the prospective family. They will then be given full details of a family which is interested in them, and can make their choice as to whether they wish to accept the position. Only when they have accepted a position are they required to pay the agency the fee of £40 plus VAT.

Universal Care works from an office in Beaconsfield, Buckinghamshire, which is open during normal office hours. It also has a 24-hour answer machine. It is licensed by the Department of Employment and is a member of the Federation of Recruitment and Employment Services.

Universale	Via Colsereno 53, 00019 Tivoli, Rome, Italy (telephone: 010 396 774 27862). Au pairs and mothers' helps are placed in Europe, particularly Italy. Wages are £35 to £200 a week depending on experience and working hours.
Verein für Internationale Jugendarbeit	39 Craven Road, London W2 3BX (telephone 071-723 0216). Places young women and men of 18 to 24 as au pairs with German families in stays of between six months to two years. Pocket money of £95–135 per month depending on experience. Basic knowledge of German essential.

9F • PAYING GUESTS AND EXCHANGE VISITS

Being a paying guest also allows one to see something of a foreign country and to learn the language while enjoying the advantages of family life. It can also profitably be combined with a course of study, and many families in fact like their guest to do something of this nature. The cost of accommodation and length of stay obviously vary considerably, and detailed information on these points is available from the agencies listed below.

A home-to-home exchange is a cheaper way of taking part in the everyday life of a family abroad, and allows one to return their hospitality. Some of the agencies can arrange visits of this kind. *Home from Home* (£6.99 plus 1.50 postage and packing), published by the Central Bureau, gives further details of exchanges and paying guest visits.

Exchange visits are normally between two young people of a similar age and educational background. They usually spend between two and six weeks in each other's homes. A paying guest lives as a member of the family, and pays for doing so. Exchanges that are 'free' are generally based on a return visit, instead of a 'one-way' guest visit.

Youth For Understanding (YFU) International Exchange was established in 1951 as a private, non-profit organisation in order to promote international understanding and world peace. YFU's core programme is an exchange experience for students between 15 and 18 years

Youth For Understanding

of age. The selected students are invited to spend a year in another country, where they live with volunteer host families and share in the new culture through personal involvement in the home, the local school and the community. Programme offerings generally include academic year programmes.

The organisation has developed a strategy that guarantees to both parties involved in the exchange the support they need.

In addition to the core programme, Youth For Understanding has developed smaller, specialised programmes. Sport For Understanding exchanges athletes and sports teams who have similar interests.

As the idea of a global village grows, it is not only young people who want to have an international experience. Youth For Understanding has launched a programme for adults as well, called Citizens For Understanding. Groups of people – often families – participate in one-week exchanges with people from another continent.

In total, YFU presently operates some 150 exchange programmes involving over 8,000 participants yearly.

An international centre in Washington DC co-ordinates a network of more than 30 partner organisations in Europe, Eurasia, North America, Latin America, Asia and the Pacific, with the involvement of some 250 employees, several thousand volunteers and more than 150,000 alumni.

YFU has developed a number of special scholarship programmes supported by the Japanese, Finnish, German and US governments. Currently more than 60 corporations from all over the world provide full and partial scholarships for over 400 YFU students yearly. Fees paid by the students' parents or obtained by community fundraising provide 85 per cent of the programme's revenues.

An elected International Advisory Council offers recommendations on programmes and financial issues to reflect the concerns of the worldwide YFU organisations. The International Board of Trustees offers guidance and support.

For further information, contact Youth For Understanding at one of the following addresses. The UK office will be able to give you contacts not listed here for the following countries:

Denmark, Finland, Greece, The Netherlands, Norway, Portugal, Sweden, Switzerland.

Belgium
YFU – Vlaanderen
Defacqzstraat 1 bus
1050 Brussels
Belgium
Telephone: + 322 534 1244

France
Exchanges et Jeunesse – YFU
9 Passage Geffroy Didelot
75017 Paris
France
Telephone: + 331 43 87 59 84

Germany
Deutsches YFU Komitee EV
Averhoffstrasse 10
2000 Hamburg 76
Germany
Telephone: + 49 40 227 0020

+ indicates international dialling code 010

Spain
Youth For Understanding
Moreto 5 (1° Izda)
28014 Madrid
Spain
Telephone: + 341 420 14 61

United Kingdom
Youth For Understanding
74 Stewarton Drive
Cambuslang
Glasgow G72 8DG
Telephone: 041 641 5294

International Secretariat
Youth For Understanding Inc
International Secretariat
3501 Newark Street NW
Washington DC 20016
USA
Telephone: + 1 202 895 1133

+ indicates international dialling code 010

Students International Lodgings Exchange (STILE)
9 rue Charcot, 92200 Neuilly/Seine, Paris, France. STILE operates in 200 universities and centres of further education in more than 50 countries, including parts of western Europe, Asia, Africa, South America, Australia, New Zealand and Israel. STILE helps to arrange exchanges of lodgings between students during vacations or studies. The individual contacts a member in a directory to make the necessary arrangements.

Anglo-Austrian Society, 46 Queen Anne's Gate, London SW1H 9AU (telephone: 071-222 0366).
The Anglo-Austrian Society organises school exchanges

and youth group travel. It also organises German language courses in Austria and can arrange travel to many European destinations.

En Famille Overseas, Old Stables, 60b Maltravers Street, Arundel, Sussex BN8 9BG (telephone: 0903 883266).
Arranges stays for paying guests in most European countries and package holidays that include language courses in France.

Florentina Bureau, 9 Tower Road, Orpington, Kent BR6 0SG (telephone: 0689 22875).
Arranges stays for paying guests in France and Germany.

Host and Guest Service Limited, Harwood House, 27 Effie Road, London SW6 1EN (telephone: 071-731 5340).
Arranges stays for paying guests in France and other European countries.

9G • STUDY COURSES AND SCHOLARSHIPS

There are many study courses available abroad, too many to be included in a book of this size. We have concentrated on selecting some courses of particular relevance to those between school and higher education, and on giving a list of useful addresses and sources of information.

A few comments from students who have followed courses abroad may be of interest here:

'I spent four months at the University of Neuchâtel in Switzerland doing a French course. Anyone with A-levels (mine were in science) can do the course, which leads to a certificate if you do the full year. Otherwise you can do various exams separately. I would recommend Neuchâtel to anyone wanting to learn some French (either at the university or at the Ecole de Commerce; the latter is much stricter and you have to turn up for lessons, do homework, etc; at the university you go or not entirely as you please) and have a good time. There is skiing close by during winter and the lake in summer, and lots of young people of all nationalities.'

'I attended the Goethe Institute, one of a large number of popular centres for the study of German, at Köchel am See from July to August. Advance booking is necessary (more than six months) if one wants to go in summer. The Institute teaches German from beginners' level upwards. There are about 23 hours of teaching a week. As a beginner I felt I learnt a lot, though some who knew German before coming didn't notice much change. The number in my class was 13 to 14 (the average). In southern Bavaria, where I

stayed, there was ample opportunity to travel around. Included in the cost is living in rented accommodation – often two in a room and one meal a day. An excursion might also be included. Grants may be obtained from the German government and other bodies. Information about this course can be obtained from the German Cultural Institute.'

'I went to the Hebrew University in Jerusalem on a seven-month programme organised by the Friends of the Hebrew University. It included Hebrew lessons, cheap accommodation on the campus and the opportunity to join university activities and attend lectures. Altogether it was a most rewarding and enjoyable experience.'

'I went to Israel to take part in an International Summer Science Institute at the Weizmann Institute of Science in Rehovot. This is a course for school-leavers from seven or eight countries, predominantly from the USA. It lasted for three intensive weeks of lectures, tutorials and practical work. This was followed by a two-week guided tour of the country and one week during which students could work on a kibbutz, on an archaeological dig, take part in a field course on desert or lake ecology, etc. The course itself was rather disappointing, mainly through my over-high expectations: not much can really be achieved in a three-week course, assuming a far lower level of scientific knowledge than was possessed by the English participants. However, I cannot overstress the value and enjoyment of the opportunity to meet science students of a similar age from other countries, and touring such a fascinating country as Israel in their company.'

Spring and summer courses are organised by AHA (Art History Abroad): they concentrate on aspects of art history, and are based in London, Rome, Florence and Venice. The courses generally last for six weeks.

Art history courses

Accommodation is in hotels; fees include return flight, travel between cities, accommodation, lectures and seminars. Apply to AHA Courses Ltd, c/o Prioryfield House, 20 Canon Street Taunton, Somerset TA1 1SW (telephone: 0823 271072).

| Austria | **Austrian Institute**, 28 Rutland Gate, London SW7 1PQ (telephone: 071-584 8653). |

Austrian Institute, 28 Rutland Gate, London SW7 1PQ (telephone: 071-584 8653).
Austrian National Tourist Office, 30 St George Street, London W1 (telephone: 071-629 0461).
Österreichische Komitee für Internationalen Studienaustausch (ÖKISTA) (Austrian Committee for International Educational Exchange) Garnisongasse 7, 1090 Vienna, Austria (telephone: 010 431 401 48/225 or 226).
Österreichische Hochschülerschaft (Austrian National Union of Students, Liechtensteinstrasse 13, 1090 Vienna (telephone: 010 43 1 310 8880).

Belgium **Belgian Embassy Cultural Department**, 103 Eaton Square, London SW1W 9AB (telephone: 071-235 5422).

Canada **Canadian Bureau for International Education***, 1400, 85 Albert Street, Ontario, Ottawa, K1P 6A4, Canada (telephone: 010 1613 237 4820).
Canadian High Commission*, Public Affairs Inquiry Office, Canada House, Trafalgar Square, London SW1Y 5BJ (telephone: 071-629 9492).

Denmark **Danish Embassy**, 55 Sloane Street, London SW1 (telephone: 071-235 1255).

Finland **Cultural Attaché, Embassy of Finland**, 38 Chesham Place, London SW1X 8HW (telephone: 071-235 9531).
Finnish Institute, 35–36 Eagle Street, London WC1R 4AP (telephone: 071-404 3309).

Service Culturel, French Embassy*, 23 Cromwell Road,   **France**
London SW7 2EL (telephone: 071-581 5292). For information enclose a large sae.
French Government Tourist Office, 178 Piccadilly, London W1V 0AL (telephone: 071-499 6911).

Young Travellers
For information regarding working holidays and learning French in France, please contact the French Embassy, Cultural Department, 22 Wilton Crescent, London SW1X 8SB (enclosing an sae).

Cultural Department, German Embassy*, 23 Belgrave   **Germany**
Square, London SW1X 8PZ (telephone: 071-235 5033). Enclose a large sae.
German Academic Exchange Service*, 17 Bloomsbury Square, London WC1A 2LP (telephone: 071-404 4065). Supplies a list of language courses and university vacation courses.
Goethe Institute*, 50 Prince's Gate, Exhibition Road, London SW7 2PH (telephone: 071-411 3400). Publishes details of German language courses run by the Goethe Institute in London and Germany.

Greek Embassy*, 1a Holland Park, London W11 3TP.   **Greece**
For information on courses in Greece, call the Embassy's education department on 071-221 0093.
Greek National Tourist Organisation, 4 Conduit Street, London W1R 0DJ (telephone: 071-734 5997).

Irish Embassy, 17 Grosvenor Place, London SW1X 7HR   **Ireland**
(telephone: 071-235 2171).

The Cultural Department, Embassy of Israel*, 2 Palace   **Israel**
Green Road, London W8 4QB (telephone: 071-957 9537).
Friends of the Hebrew University of Jersualem, 3 St John's

Wood Road, London NW8 8RB (telephone: 071-286 1176). The School for Overseas Students at the University offers a five-month course from February to June for students between school and university. Summer courses are run in a wide variety of subjects including Arabic, Hebrew and Yiddish. One-year courses include a programme of Jewish, Israel and Middle East studies, and a postgrad course (in English) at the Faculty of Social Science and Humanities.

Italy   **Italian Institute***, 3a Belgrave Square, London SW1X 8NX (telephone 071-235 1461).
John Hall Pre-university Interim Course, 12 Gainsborough Road, Ipswich, Suffolk IP4 2UR (telephone 0473 251223). The courses are on European civilisation, especially the visual arts and music, for non-specialists. They include practical options – languages, drawing, painting and photography. Spring course in Venice £3,150, with optional extra periods in Florence and Rome.

Luxemburg   **The Secretary, Embassy of Luxemburg** , 27 Wilton Crescent, London SW1X 8SD (telephone: 071-235 6961). Lists of student organisations and educational courses are available. Send an sae.
Luxemburg National Tourist Office, 36–37 Piccadilly, London W1V 9PA (telephone: 071-434 2800).

Netherlands   Short-term employment **The Director General for Manpower**, Visseringlaan 25, 2288 ER Rijswijk, The Netherlands (telephone: 010 31 70 130911).

Norway   **Counsellor for Press and Culture**, Royal Norwegian Embassy*, 25 Belgrave Square, London SW1X 8QD (telephone: 071-235 7151).

Poland

Polish Cultural Institute*, 34 Portland Place, London W1N 4HQ (telephone: 071-636 6032).
Polish Tourist Information Centre, 82 Mortimer Street, London W1N 7DE (telephone: 071-580 8028).

Portugal

Full EC passport holders have 90 days to register with the Servico de Esgrangeiros. Each major city will have this department.

Russia

Intourist Moscow Ltd, Intourist House, 219 Marsh Wall, Isle of Dogs, London E14 9FJ (telephone: 071-538 8600). Courses in Moscow and St Petersburg only.

Spain

Hispanic and Luso-Brazilian Council*, 2 Belgrave Square, London SW1X 8PJ (telephone: 071-235 2303). Information leaflets are available on study courses and opportunities in Spain and Latin America. £2 each plus p&p.
Spanish Institute, 102 Eaton Square, London SW1W 9AN (telephone: 071-235 1484).
Spanish National Tourist Office, 57 St James's Street, London SW1 (telephone: 071-499 0901).

Sweden

Cultural Attaché, Swedish Embassy*, 11 Montague Place, London W1H 2AL (telephone: 071-724 2101).

Switzerland

Swiss National Tourist Office*, Swiss Centre, New Coventry Street, London W1V 8EE (telephone: 071-734 1921).

USA

Council on International Educational Exchange (CIEE)*, 205 East 42nd Street, New York, NY 10017, USA.
The English-Speaking Union of the Commonwealth, Dartmouth House, 37 Charles Street, London W1X 8AB (telephone: 071-493 3328), offers scholarships for school-leavers to spend one year in North American independent schools. There are also awards for two terms only,

beginning immediately after Christmas. Students must be of high academic ability and parents are asked to pay return fares and incidental expenses.

US Embassy, 24 Grosvenor Square, London W1A 1AE. For information on courses in the USA, call the Embassy on 071-499 9000 and ask for the US information service on ext 2925. You must call between 10 am and noon. Information on current vacancies and possibilities can be obtained by contacting the Personnel Office.

* Indicates that information on study courses is available on request.

Worldwide   Youth for Understanding, 74 Stewarton Drive. Cambuslang, Glasgow G72 8DG (telephone: 041-641 5294), for 15 to 19 year-olds wishing to learn about another culture by living with a family abroad, becoming involved in the local community, and attending a local school. There are presently some 150 exchange programmes with an average number of 8,000 participants each year. Both full and partial scholarships are available as well full fee-paying exchanges.

Further   *Study Abroad*, published by UNESCO and obtainable
information   from HMSO, gives details of international scholarships and courses. Price £14.95. Available from HMSO Books, 51 Nine Elms Lane, London SW8 5DT (telephone: 071-873 0011).

Study Holidays has details of all language courses around Europe. It is intended for those who wish to improve their language skills, whether it be in preparation for examinations or simply from a desire to learn more about other countries. Price £7.95 plus £1.50 p&p. Available from the Central Bureau for Educational Visits and Exchanges, Seymour Mews, London W1H 9PE (telephone: 071-486 5101).

9H • TRAVEL, EXPEDITIONS AND ADVENTURE

Travel abroad is expensive, but all young people between the ages of 16 and 30 who are in full-time education are eligible for an International Student or Scholar Identity Card (ISIC), which will entitle them to reductions on travel fares and on charges of admission to museums and galleries, etc, abroad. An application for an ISIC must be accompanied by (i) valid proof of full-time scholar status (eg a formal letter of certification from one's school or college, with an official stamp, or a National Union of Students' membership card); (ii) a passport photograph, signed on the back; (iii) full names; (iv) date of birth; (v) nationality. ISIC cards are obtainable from local student travel bureaux or from the Anglo-Austrian Society (address below). Information about student travel can be obtained from the following organisations:

Anglo-Austrian Society

Anglo-Austrian Society, 46 Queen Anne's Gate, London SW1H 9AU (telephone: 071-222 0366 or 071-222 2430). Besides specialising in travel to Austria, the Society can also book budget flights to selected European destinations including Munich, Zurich, Budapest and Prague. The society also offers German language courses in Austria for young people aged 15 and over, as well as school exchanges and youth group travel.

Inter-Rail

British Rail's Inter-Rail ticket, available to anyone under the age of 26, entitles the holder to one month's free travel in 19 European countries and Morocco. If obtained in Britain it also provides a reduction of a third on travel in the UK.

For the adventurous, 'time off' can be a once-in-a-lifetime chance to taste the rewards and hardships of exploration.

Experiments | **The Experiment in International Living** (EIL) is a non-profit-making educational travel association founded in 1932 in the USA. The first programme involved a group of Americans spending a summer 'experiment' living in Switzerland and Germany; hence the name.

The aims of EIL are to promote greater peace, understanding and friendship between people in different parts of the world. This aim is largely achieved by arranging for participants to spend a period (known as a 'home-stay') living in the home of a host in one of many countries around the world and through their kibbutz programme.

Some of EIL's programmes are linked with language courses and study overseas. For example, it is possible to study French in France whilst living with a French family. Other programmes are presented as a 'more exciting and adventurous' alternative to a package holiday. EIL programmes typically last for a period of between one and four weeks.

A fee is charged for participation in all EIL programmes. For example, a four-week homestay in France currently costs £470. This fee covers accommodation costs and the services of a local EIL representative. However, the costs of travel and insurance are not included and these must be arranged and paid for by the participant.

EIL host families are specially selected for their willingness to welcome foreigners into their homes and share their way of life. Participants must be friendly and flexible and prepared to adapt to conditions locally, which in many places are more basic than those at home. The age limit for participants is 16–70.

EIL also operates an au pair programme offering 12 month stays in the USA or Canada. The age limit is 18–25 and applicants should be non-smokers with a full driving licence. For these programmes a wage is paid and a free return flight and insurance are included.

Further details can be obtained from EIL Limited, 'Otesaga', West Malvern Road, Malvern, Worcestershire WR14 4EN (telephone: 0684 562577). Details of EIL organisations in other countries are given on pages 159–162.

WEXAS International Ltd

Contact 45–49 Brompton Road, London SW3 1DE (telephone: 071-589 0500/3315). Makes awards totalling £2,000 to approved group expeditions through the Royal Geographical Society Award Scheme. Members of WEXAS benefit from special rates for immunisation, flights, insurance, hotels and car hire, as well as having access to Discoverers' holidays and receiving Traveller magazine. WEXAS also publishes the *Traveller's Handbook* (available at discount to members), which gives practical hints for all independent travellers and lists many useful names and addresses. The price is £11.95 and it is available in bookshops.

Further information

Adventure Holidays, £5.95, published by Vacation Work, 9 Park End Street, Oxford OX1 1HJ, is a guide to the opportunities and pitfalls of travel in over 100 countries. *Work Your Way Around the World* is available from the same publishers at £9.95.

The International Youth Hostel Handbook, available from any Youth Hostel Adventure Shop. Volume 1 gives addresses and brief details of hostels in Europe and the Mediterranean. Volume 2 gives information about hostels in Africa, Asia, the USA and Australasia.

NOTES

HARD CASH!
A Student Helpbook Title

This lively and informative guide to financing higher education is ideal for students thinking of going to college, who are worried about surviving financially.

Part 1 explains all the sources of money students should be aware of and tap into: grants, awards, sponsorship, covenants, Access Funds, Student Loans, Career Development Loans and more.

Part 2 shows how twenty-one students in Britain and the US have followed in the American tradition of self-sufficiency by working part-time or by setting up their own businesses while still at college.

Individual student stories demonstrate such projects as:

- A catering company called 'Simply Stuffed' providing food for college society receptions
- A tourist guide service round St Andrews in Scotland
- A babysitting service for the children of college tutors
- A dress hire agency
- Windsurfing lessons in the North Sea.

Even now, when jobs are so scarce, part-time and holiday work is available if you know where to look for it. These stories will point you in the right direction.

STUDENT HELPBOOK SERIES

This series of advice publications is designed to help students of all ages make the right choices about their careers and education. The books' animated text and cartoons make them a lively read for students who want to take their own decisions. Many careers teachers, advisers and parents find them an invaluable source of reference. The titles marked with an asterisk have been recommended by the Department of Employment for its Careers Library Initiative, a scheme designed to provide schools and colleges with first-rate careers information.

Titles in the series include

- A Year Off ... A Year On?
- Decisions at 13/14+*
- Decisions at 15/16+*
- Decisions at 17/18+*
- Your Choice of A-levels
- Matters of Degree
- Hard Cash!
- Excel at Interviews
- Jobs and Careers after A-levels*

If you would like to order any of these titles, please contact Biblios Publishers' Distribution Services, Star Road, Partridge Green, West Sussex RH13 8LD (tel: 0403 710851).

For general information contact our Customer Services Department, Hobsons Publishing PLC, Bateman Street, Cambridge CB2 1LZ (tel: 0223 354551).